I0014937

Converting procedural code to object oriented code in Java

Dedicated to my wife Kamini Kumari

Author information

For any help please contact :
Amazon Author Page :
amazon.com/author/ajaykumar
Email : ajaycucek@gmail.com ,
ajaxreso@gmail.com
Linkedin :
https://www.linkedin.com/in/ajaycucek
Facebook :
https://www.facebook.com/ajaycucek
Youtube :
https://www.youtube.com/channel/UC1uXE
ebtqCLYxVdzirKZGIA
Twitter : https://twitter.com/ajaycucek
Instagram :
https://www.instagram.com/ajaycucek/
Skype : ajaycucek

Table of contents

Module 1 : Book Overview

Book Overview

Welcome to my book, Converting procedural code to object oriented code in Java. I am a senior software developer and part of my work involves reviewing other people's code. But I find funny is that most of the code I read is really not the object oriented. It is rather procedural, with classes and modules only being the former containers of code.

- How to avoid branching
- How to never use a null reference
- How to encapsulate object's state

Well, in this book, we're going to show what it takes to write through object or into code.

You'll see how to avoid branching, especially around the boolean and the knowledge. You will learn how to never use null reference and how to encapsulate objects, state and expose behavior. By the end of this book, you will be able to recognize your own errors of the past and develop a better coding style before beginning the book. You should be familiar with such concepts as polymorphism, inheritance and similar. You should feel at home with Java, like having no second thoughts about control structures or functional interface is, for example, from here you should be able to dive into advanced book on object oriented programming and design.

Module 2 : Attaining Extensibility with Object-oriented Code

What Makes Code Object-oriented?

In this book "making your Java code more object oriented", I plan to show you many examples which can be re factored and redesigned. So there's more of the object oriented concepts take part in their final design. Why would we want to do that? You may ask. Applying object orientation doesn't come without the price. In order to begin valued object orientation, we must understand its benefits first. Note, however, that we could write object oriented coding languages like C if we wanted to. It is even possible to write assembler Macron's that enable writing entirely object oriented assembly code. That proves that object orientation doesn't necessarily come from the programming language. It rather comes from a mind shift, and that is how the journey begins. C++ and Objective See were the first widely used. The language is that applied these ideas, but they had only created an impression off objects they were not true object or into the languages. Early on, Java and C Sharp started as object or intense straight up. They have also adopted function or paradigm later, that should be noted. And yet we still see those old structured programing. Practice is all around. I often find blame, see code when I review code in other companies. Even the most recent textbooks on Java programming offered that same kind of playing C code wrapped in two classes. For the great part of my own career, I did it the same way all until it finally dawned on me I changed my mind, and now my coding style is different. The problem with the old me and the problem is so many other programmers was that I never really appreciated the principal's off object oriented programming at that time. It is not that inheritance polymorphism encapsulation stuff that is just a facade. Understanding, object oriented paradigm means to go deeper under the surface and see it in its bear form. It takes a master to define objects and attain encapsulation and true polymorphic behavior off objects. Everything yes, comes naturally. Then when you see it that way, you will understand that a true engine, which delivers power to the object oriented paradigm, remains in those two almost trivial pieces that make everything else fit together. So mitri that this pointer in every instance level method Cole and dynamic dispatch, which lets your substitute one concrete function implementation for another at runtime without disturbing the caller. Before we start with concrete code, let me quickly list the topics that we will cover during this book. By the end of this, we will also see a few examples which demonstrated the basic ideas, and after that we will already be running at full speed for code samples, turning them into object oriented.

What Follows in this book

- **Introduction** : A collection is an object. A missing object is also an object.
- **Branching on Booleans** : Replace branching with polymorphic calls.
- **Immutable objects** : How to avoid bugs due to mutability.
- **Avoiding nulls** : Null is not an object.
- **Optional<T> type** : No more nulls in business applications

I assumed that at this point we all agree that object or into the code is what we want to have In the end, let me then briefly show what you will learn in this book. In this introductory module, you will only see a few lines of code to tickle your imagination. You will see that a collection off objects is also an object, and you will see that even the missing object can be turned into a proper object which mothers the sentence I'm missing. After that, we will straighten up and starts on serious programming. You will learn how boolean flags are ruining the design. We will talk about branching the infamous see fell's instruction. You will learn how polymorphic book can replace many explicit branching instructions. After that, we will talk about the mutable objects and value type semantic. You will see the dangerous that mutability

6

incurs the design and how small immutable objects can help overcome the problems. We will then turn our attention to the wretched and null references. No is not an object designed that incorporates nuts is not object oriented. You will see designs that can substitute many. Null references for those knows that cannot be replaced. Using these designs, we will turn to the option or type from Java. Eight. That knowledge will help you remove all null references and replace them with proper and safe objects. I hope you will stay with me for this book. I will advise you not to jump over modules. This book is not a manual on object oriented programming. To be a good, object oriented programmer, you need to understand the reasons why those principles were made that way and what benefits we get when we applied them. I will do my best to explain that backing story for this book. Let's get onto it done with two simple examples.

An Example that Lacks Objects

One way to show you why we need more object orientation is to see pieces of coat that are lacking it. Throughout this book, I will be using Intelligence Community Edition. You can use any code editor in which you feel comfortable. That should not affect the outcome. All code in this book is compliant with Java eight and, of course, in a later edition.

```java
public class Main {
    public int sum(int[] values) {
        int sum = 0;

        for (int value: values) {
            sum += value;
        }

        return sum;
    }

    public static void main(String[] args) {

    }
}
```

Look at this function. It is bad. You might not know what it means for a piece of code to be great, but you can easily tell allows you won what makes this a bad code sample. Then it's summing up the numbers. What can go wrong with that? Well, it lacks flexibility and flexibility is on top of the list of any customers. Expectations. One day, the customer says, summing up is good, but I only want odd numbers in fine, we may say, Here you are.

```java
public class Main {
    public int sum(int[] values) {
        int sum = 0;

        for (int value: values) {
            if (value % 2 != 0) {
                sum += value;
            }
        }

        return sum;
    }

    public static void main(String[] args) {

    }
}
```

These are just the old numbers, but then the customer says all right. But I only want all the numbers sometimes not every time. Right, Ah, boolean flag will do it, and it did the job. But now it is already clear that this is the wrong way to make things done. What if the customer wants even numbers next or every other number? No matter whether it is even a rod, this way of solving the problem won't work. In the long run, the solution will grow large and complicated. I won't be able to maintain it, let alone that it will be impossible to tell whether the code is correct in the first place. If we have settled down saying that this code is bad, how can we tell what exactly is wrong with it? The short answer is that it is lacking dynamic dispatch The selection criterion before summation must be dynamic. Right now the decision is

static, hard coded in the middle of the low.
Customers often change their mind but this
structure doesn't support the change. By
changing this code will risk breaking some
other future. You don't want to change
behavior by changing code. You want to
change behavior by substituting an object.
This solution is bad because it lacks objects.

```java
public class Main {
    public int sum(int[] values, selector) {
        int sum = 0;

        for (int value: selector.applyTo(values)) {
            sum += value;
        }

        return sum;
    }

    public static void main(String[] args) {

    }
}
```

For example, a selector. I don't know what
this sees yet, so this code won't compile. The
selector will give me the numbers to some.
Does this look better now? that we have an
object which represents the selector. We can
suddenly support different requirements,
even the crazy ones. That is great. Substitute
a new selector for the prior one and a
completely different subset of values will be
summed up. Then what's the story about this
array with numbers? Why the array? I
wanted to behave like an object to. I wanted

to be able to sum up its content using the dynamic selector. Then why this whole function?

```
public class Main {
    public int sum(int[] values, selector) {
        return values.sum(selector);
    }

    public static void main(String[] args) {

    }
}
```

If the arrays a proper object and it knows how to apply the selector, then what's the purpose of this entire method? During this book, you will learn that operations should not be implemented at the consuming end. This class here is the consumer. It needs a specific sum of values from an array. This glass should not sum up the numbers. It should ask some object to produce the sum for it. And now that I have indeed done that, I can delete this matter than Tyree. This class will focus on its own responsibilities not on filtering and adding numbers.

```
public class Main {
    public static void main(String[] args) {

    }
}
```

Now the code looks better, right? I mean, there is no code. This is the perfect solution with the some solution defined on an array and with the selection criterion built into the selector class, the whole solution will magically become object oriented. As a result, it has become trivial to use and fully extensible, This code supports future requirements out of the box.

Putting Objects Where It Doesn't Look Possible

```
public class Main {
    public void showIt(String data) {
        String upper;
        if (data == null) {
            upper = null;
        }
        else {
            upper = data.toUpperCase();
        }
        System.out.println(upper);
    }

    public static void main(String[] args) {

    }
}
```

Take a look at another example. It is so typical to right, if else instructions around now conditions even today. I mean, we are far into the 21st century, and we're still branching around null references. Isn't there anything better? This function receives a string and tries to print it's uppercase version to the concept, but a string can be now, and we must not call. It's too uppercase method. We're branching around another reference, because it could happen that we don't have an object. There it is again, no object. Only this time it's a bit different compared to previous example. This time we do have a class, but we don't have any instance of that class. Here is the problem. In really life, you cannot have nothing. If you don't have an ice cream, then you simply don't have it. You cannot not eat an ice cream, which you don't have. Wow code doesn't work that way. In programming, even nothing is something. You're perfectly safe to construct an object, which is nothing. Let's doubt that the string might not be there. Call this object class, maybe string. Maybe it's a string. Maybe it's nothing.

```
public class Main {
    public void showIt(MaybeString data) {
        MaybeString upper = data.toUpperCase();
        String toPrint = upper.orElse( substitute: "");
        System.out.println(toPrint);
    }

    public static void main(String[] args) {

    }
}
```

I don't know in advance I want to turn that into upper case. Maybe. I mean, only if it is there. I don't want to turn it to upper case. If it is nothing off course that now turning a maybe string to uppercase can only maybe produce an uppercase string. Do you like this? This may be strength classes thinking for me If there is the string, please give it back to me. Turned to upper case. If there is nothing, please feel free to give me nothing in return. I'm fine with that. If I wanted to print it out, I needed a truth spring. I must tell what the string will be if it didn't exist Now that I have collapsed it to a proper string. I don't need these branching structure anymore. And I can simply print that resulting string out. They're no nuts in this code. They're only objects as the consequence. All transformations are unconditional. I won't be pushing examples any further than this in this introductory module. The rest of the book will be much more elaborate and much closer to really world applications. In fact, all examples in this course have been taken from really applications before stepping forward. Let's briefly summarize this module

Summary

In this module, you could see the basic motivation that stands behind efforts to write object oriented code. It pays to keep that motivation alive. Despite all the troubles we normally endure while developing applications for the real world, it pays to stick with the principles off object oriented program because that will improve the ability of our applications to survive in the real world.

In this course you will learn to:
- Detect where objects are missing
- Avoid branching around Booleans
- Remove null references
- Apply principles of object-oriented programming

In this book, you will learn how to detect the lack off object orientation in a design and then how to overcome that shortcoming. You will see techniques to avoid branching instructions and replace them with polymorphic calls on objects. You will also learn how to remove all null references from code. By the end of this book, you will be equipped to it. Principal knowledge off object oriented programming. If you're ready, we can start digging for some real code. In the next module, we will see that boolean flags and branching around them are completely unnecessary in object oriented code

Module 3 : Rendering Branching over Boolean Flags Obsolete

Introducing the Problem in Code

In so many cases, we start happily with a small and coherent class, which is doing one thing and doing it right. Then new requirements come, and our class gradually erodes into a blob of code that cannot be maintained anymore. In this module, we will keep complexity in check by turning the branching logic into explicit state objects. Go this telling more than words.

```java
public class Account {
    public void deposit(BigDecimal amount) {

    }

    public void withdraw(BigDecimal amount) {

    }
```

This class is modeling a money account, allowing deposits and withdrawals that is rare. Requirements begin. We're free to call the deposit method whenever we want. But in order to withdraw money from an account, holder must verify their identity in some other way.

```java
public class Account {
    private boolean isVerified;

    public void holderVerified() {
        this.isVerified = true;
    }

    public void deposit(BigDecimal amount) {

    }

    public void withdraw(BigDecimal amount) {
        if (!this.isVerified)
            return;   // Or do something more :
        // Withdraw money
    }
}
```

Traditional approach would be to track whether the holder has been verified. Now we can stop invalid with Rollo by branching over the ease verified value. This was easy, right?

```java
public class Account {
    private boolean isVerified;
    private boolean isClosed;

    public void holderVerified() {
        this.isVerified = true;
    }

    public void closeAccount() {
        this.isClosed = true;
    }

    public void deposit(BigDecimal amount) {
        if (this.isClosed)
            return;   // Or do something more meaningful
        // Deposit money
    }

    public void withdraw(BigDecimal amount) {
        if (!this.isVerified)
            return;   // Or do something more meaningful
        if (this.isClosed)
            return;
        // Withdraw money
    }
}
```

But don't celebrate yet. Here's another request coming our way. Holder can close the account when the account is closed. The user cannot deposit. Nor can they withdraw money, more branching on the way. No deposits after one more branching over the boolean flag and doing one thing or the other. Depending on the outcome, it goes the same with the withdrawal. The problem with this solution is that a code which is testing the accounts state is explicit. Why should we consider that a bad thing you may ask. Well, explicit condition tests are making our code

complicated. For one thing, let me show you what I mean.

```java
public class Account {
    private boolean isVerified;
    private boolean isClosed;
    private BigDecimal balance;

    public Account() {
        this.balance = BigDecimal.ZERO;
    }

    public void holderVerified() {
        this.isVerified = true;
    }

    public void closeAccount() {
        this.isClosed = true;
    }

    public void deposit(BigDecimal amount) {
        if (this.isClosed)
            return;   // Or do something more meaningful
        this.balance = this.balance.add(amount);
    }
    public void withdraw(BigDecimal amount) {
        if (!this.isVerified)
            return;   // Or do something more meaningful
        if (this.isClosed)
            return;
        this.balance = this.balance.subtract(amount);
    }
}
```

I'm gonna just add balanced on the account for simplicity. I'm not keeping record of the currency. You should never create a balance variable without the associated currents in real projects. Introduce a money type to make balance and currency live together forever off. After in the deposit method, I

will simply increase the band's. Once again. The implementation is oversimplified. For the purpose of this demo withdrawal will also be affected. I want test whether current balance is sufficient for now. In this demonstration, I will keep focused on operations that are changing state of the money account, and the state will be changed in terms that the balance will now be lower than it used to be. Now that we have a couple of features in the class, we come to the question that has been bothering me all the way long. How many ways there are to execute the deposit method? There are two ways One is to drop for this if instruction, and just exit the method that happens if the account is closed and other ways to pass the test and increase the balance.

Test case #1

Deposit 10.00
Close
Deposit 1.00
Assert balance = 10.00

Test case #2

Deposit 10.00
Deposit 1.00
Assert balance = 11.00

If we wanted to test this account class, then we would have to write two tests for the deposit method.

Test case #3

Deposit 10.00
Withdraw 1.00
Assert balance = 10.00

Test case #4

Deposit 10.00
Verify holder, close
Withdraw 1.00
Assert balance = 10.00

Test case #5

Deposit 10.00
Verify holder
Withdraw 1.00
Assert balance = 9.00

And how about the withdrawal method? We need one test to make sure that the balance remains the same. If Holder was not verified with, the DRO should be silently rejected. Another test to make sure that balance remains unchanged when the account holder is indeed verified. But account has been closed after that balance remains unchanged again. Finally, we need 3rd test to make sure that the balance did change. If Holder was verified, an account was not closed before

21

**withdrawing the money. All in all, it takes
five tests to demonstrate that these two
methods of their count costs are working as
expected.**

```java
public class Account {
    private boolean isVerified;
    private boolean isClosed;
    private boolean isFrozen;
    private BigDecimal balance;

    private AccountUnfrozen onUnfrozen;

    public Account(AccountUnfrozen onUnfrozen) {
        this.balance = BigDecimal.ZERO;
        this.onUnfrozen = onUnfrozen;
    }

    public void holderVerified() {
        this.isVerified = true;
    }

    public void closeAccount() {
        this.isClosed = true;
    }

    public void freezeAccount() {
        if (this.isClosed)
            return; // Account must not be closed
        if (!this.isVerified)
            return; // Account must be verified first
        this.isFrozen = true;
    }
}
```

```
public void deposit(BigDecimal amount) {
    if (this.isClosed)
        return;   // Or do something more meaningful
    if (this.isFrozen) {
        this.isFrozen = false;
        this.onUnfrozen.handle();
    }
    this.balance = this.balance.add(amount);
}

public void withdraw(BigDecimal amount) {
    if (!this.isVerified)
        return;   // Or do something more meaningful
    if (this.isClosed)
        return;
    this.balance = this.balance.subtract(amount);
}
}
```

And what about the new requirements? Banks often put some accounts on ice, especially to indicate that the account was not actively used for some period of time. Another flag has been added about the freeze account method puts the account of frozen state, but only if it is not blows are unverifiable. That is how the customer wanted it, and that was not all the customer wanted from us. Depositing money should automatically unfreeze the account, but when the account gets a liquid again, it must call certain callback function defined on this account. Unfrozen interface, I already feel, is being tortured by my customers. More state will pour into the account costs. The verbosity off this class is becoming unbearable. The code back is initialized for the constructor, and I haven't even started developing behavior. Depositing will change in case that the account was frozen. Watch carefully and see how implementation is gradually becoming complicated. As more requirements are being added, deposit must guarantee to unfreeze any frozen account. But then another branching comes because the callback must not be involved on every deposit, but only if the account was frozen before it. When the account is frozen, it should immediately get unfrozen. Do you see the complexity sneaking into the class? And it's only going to get worse as more requirements arrive. You can bet on that. This latest changes asking for even more test cases. The sixth test case will demonstrate that the callback was indeed in hoped at the airport. In time test case number seven proves that previously frozen account is unfrozen. After a deposit, more tests come to mind, like one proving that the callback was not invoked. If the account was not frozen, eight tested this far. And what about the withdrawal method? Blatant copy and paste? I might have turned this block into a private method. Just avoid code repetition. But that will not help me emerge. Test cases. All test cases will have to be repeated on the withdrawal method with slight modifications. That is total of 11 test cases so far, and we didn't even get to thinking about testing other members of the class. By now, we have seen how bad the situation can become. If we just add branching logic with every new requirement in the remainder of this module, I will show you a simple technique to put the problem under control. It will be based on the state design pattern, but you don't have to be afraid of it. Its core state pattern is very simple. As you will see, I'll try to introduce states progressively that will help you understand gradual improvements in code.

Turning Branching into a Function

I guess that the hardest part in this implementation was that about unfreezing the account. Let's fix that part. First,

```java
public void deposit(BigDecimal amount) {
    if (this.isClosed)
        return;   // Or do something more meaningful
    this.ensureUnfrozen();
    this.balance = this.balance.add(amount);
}

public void withdraw(BigDecimal amount) {
    if (!this.isVerified)
        return;   // Or do something more meaningful
    if (this.isClosed)
        return;
    this.ensureUnfrozen();
    this.balance = this.balance.subtract(amount);
}

private void ensureUnfrozen() {
    if (this.isFrozen) {
        this.isFrozen = false;
        this.onUnfrozen.handle();
    }
    else {
        // Do nothing
    }
}
```

I will extract a new method which will only deal with the unfreezing logic. Now comes the important step. Make sure that you are focused on what I'm just about to do. I will introduce an else branch in dis method. The reason why I'm doing this is to make the implementation symmetrical.

```java
public void deposit(BigDecimal amount) {
    if (this.isClosed)
        return;   // Or do something more meaningful
    this.ensureUnfrozen();
    this.balance = this.balance.add(amount);
}

public void withdraw(BigDecimal amount) {
    if (!this.isVerified)
        return;   // Or do something more meaningful
    if (this.isClosed)
        return;
    this.ensureUnfrozen();
    this.balance = this.balance.subtract(amount);
}

private void ensureUnfrozen() {
    if (!this.isFrozen)
        return;

    this.isFrozen = false;
    this.onUnfrozen.handle();
}
```

There's a huge difference between if and if else instructions plain if can be used as a so called guard close, This coding style is more convenient as it makes the meaning of branching more obvious. The method now begins with a guard testing whether preconditions for this matter are satisfied. Precondition to remove the frozen status is that the account is frozen. If it is not, just get out of the method and do nothing. Can you feel the change in the way I'm talking about branching? Guard clauses one thing full fledged. If else is another thing, I leave no

room for the incomplete. If instruction either guard against a non applicable case or branch execution into to this joint blocks of code, so we could say that I have started from the Guard clause form and then I have elevated it into a full flash. If house.

```java
public void withdraw(BigDecimal amount) {
    if (!this.isVerified)
        return;   // Or do something more meaningful
    if (this.isClosed)
        return;
    this.ensureUnfrozen();
    this.balance = this.balance.subtract(amount);
}

private void ensureUnfrozen() {
    if (this.isFrozen) {
        this.unfreeze();
    }
    else {
        this.stayUnfrozen();
    }
}

private void unfreeze() {
    this.isFrozen = false;
    this.onUnfrozen.handle();
}

private void stayUnfrozen() {
    // Do nothing
}
```

Now I can make it explicit that if and else branches are leading to separate blocks of code, it may surprise you to see me pulling out an empty method from an empty else

28

brand. But let me ask you a question. Now, do you see how I'm invoking this Ensure unfrozen method? What if it were a method on some other objects rather than this? What if I added an interface with that name?

```
public interface EnsureUnfrozen {
    void execute();
}
public class Account {
    private boolean isVerified;
    private boolean isClosed;
    private boolean isFrozen;
    private BigDecimal balance;

    private EnsureUnfrozen ensureUnfrozen;
    private AccountUnfrozen onUnfrozen;

    public Account(AccountUnfrozen onUnfrozen) {
        this.balance = BigDecimal.ZERO;
        this.ensureUnfrozen = this::stayUnfrozen;
        this.onUnfrozen = onUnfrozen;
    }

    public void holderVerified() {
        this.isVerified = true;
    }

    public void closeAccount() {
        this.isClosed = true;
    }

    public void freezeAccount() {
        if (this.isClosed)
            return;  // Account must not be closed
        if (!this.isVerified)
            return;  // Account must be verified first
```

29

```
public void closeAccount() {
    this.isClosed = true;
}

public void freezeAccount() {
    if (this.isClosed)
        return;    // Account must not be closed
    if (!this.isVerified)
        return; // Account must be verified first
    this.isFrozen = true;
}

public void deposit(BigDecimal amount) {
    if (this.isClosed)
        return;    // Or do something more meaningful
    this.ensureUnfrozen.execute();
    this.balance = this.balance.add(amount);
}

public void withdraw(BigDecimal amount) {
    if (!this.isVerified)
        return;    // Or do something more meaningful
    if (this.isClosed)
        return;
    this.ensureUnfrozen.execute();
    this.balance = this.balance.subtract(amount);
}
```

**The trick is to imagine that ensure unfrozen
is a separate entity, a function implemented
elsewhere. A concrete object carrying a
concrete implementation will be stored in
this field. Initially, the concrete
implementation will be to stay on frozen now
in the deposit and withdraw methods. I can
freely invoke this object. Quite cryptic way
of telling that I want to optionally unfreeze
the account. But don't worry. This is not
what the code will look like. In the end, I**

wanted to show you the flexibility which this way of thinking is bringing. What happens if the account gets frozen at some point. If someone asked for unfreezing after that, then stay on frozen method would clearly be the inappropriate target. Lucky enough, the freeze method is the only place where that change happens.

```
public void freezeAccount() {
    if (this.isClosed)
        return;   // Account must not be closed
    if (!this.isVerified)
        return; // Account must be verified first
    this.isFrozen = true;
    this.ensureUnfrozen = this::unfreeze;
}
```

I will change the ensure and frozen object to point to the other method. Instead, this will make sure that the unfreeze method is executed the next time someone wishes to ensure the account is unfrozen.

```
private void unfreeze() {
    this.isFrozen = false;
    this.onUnfrozen.handle();
    this.ensureUnfrozen = this::stayUnfrozen;
}
```

Finally, there is one more place where the change may occur in the unfreeze method itself. Once done, the right behavior will be to stay on frozen. This completes the re factoring, which renders a boolean flag and branching around it obsolete. We have turned the table and made a perfectly flat solution.

```java
public class Account {
    private boolean isVerified;
    private boolean isClosed;
    private BigDecimal balance;

    private EnsureUnfrozen ensureUnfrozen;
    private AccountUnfrozen onUnfrozen;

    public Account(AccountUnfrozen onUnfrozen) {
        this.balance = BigDecimal.ZERO;
        this.ensureUnfrozen = this::stayUnfrozen;
        this.onUnfrozen = onUnfrozen;
    }

    public void holderVerified() {
        this.isVerified = true;
    }

    public void closeAccount() {
        this.isClosed = true;
    }

    public void freezeAccount() {
        if (this.isClosed)
            return;   // Account must not be closed
        if (!this.isVerified)
            return;   // Account must be verified first
```

```java
public void deposit(BigDecimal amount) {
    if (this.isClosed)
        return;   // Or do something more meaningful
    this.ensureUnfrozen.execute();
    this.balance = this.balance.add(amount);
}

public void withdraw(BigDecimal amount) {
    if (!this.isVerified)
        return;   // Or do something more meaningful
    if (this.isClosed)
        return;
    this.ensureUnfrozen.execute();
    this.balance = this.balance.subtract(amount);
}

private void unfreeze() {
    this.onUnfrozen.handle();
    this.ensureUnfrozen = this::stayUnfrozen;
}

private void stayUnfrozen() {
    // Do nothing
}
}
```

I can remove this is frozen flag and it's using the freeze account and the entire hard coded and sure and frozen behavior. And this last usage in the UN freeze method. This re factoring was the first step in the direction of reducing complexity of the account costs. You may argue that all the code is still there. Only one branching instruction was removed, but that was not the point. Anyway, the point is in introducing a different mind process. The one we're branching is performed by selecting an object, not by selecting a block of code to execute. Stay with me a little longer and you will see what follows. The next step will be to move the entire freezing and unfreezing behavior to a separate class that will definitely simplify the account class.

Turning a Function into an Object

The ensure unfrozen object is doing the right thing whenever the account should be unfrozen. But the core problem remains as the account class still thinks about when and how to involve the operation. The time has come to remove that logic from the class entirely.

```
public interface Freezable {
    void deposit();
    void withdraw();
    void freezeAccount();
}
```

Let me define a separate type which will deal with these aspects of freezing. The purpose of this interface will be to think about how the freezing St changes, but not when that happens. These free operations are affecting the freezing state deposit withdraw and freeze account. This interface almost defines a state, I said, almost because there's one thing missing. It will become obvious when I define concrete states. For example, an active

account would be represented by the
Freezable active class.

```
public class FreezableActive implements Freezable {
    @Override
    public void deposit() {

    }

    @Override
    public void withdraw() {

    }

    @Override
    public void freezeAccount() {

    }
}
```

It would do nothing special in the deposit
and withdraw methods because it already
models the active state of the account. But
the freeze account operation would cause US
troubles as the state would have to become
frozen. An object cannot change its own
runtime type, though, when we have such a
need than we normally return.

```java
public class FreezableActive implements Freezable {
    @Override
    public void deposit() {

    }

    @Override
    public void withdraw() {

    }

    @Override
    public Freezable freezeAccount() {

    }
}
```

A new object to tell the caller that current object must be substituted another type would model the frozen state, and that object would have to turn itself into active state when deposit or withdraw is involved. That is how we come to the design in which every method of a state is returning the next state.

```java
public interface Freezable {
    Freezable deposit();
    Freezable withdraw();
    Freezable freezeAccount();
}
```

Now we can get back to implementing the active steak.

```java
public class FreezableActive implements Freezable {
    @Override
    public Freezable deposit() {
        return this;
    }

    @Override
    public Freezable withdraw() {
        return this;
    }

    @Override
    public Freezable freezeAccount() {
        return new FreezableFrozen();
    }
}
```

The 1st 2 methods will be tribunal to complete because we have nothing to do when the account is already active. Simply, the current state will remain, but the free is account method will cost us some thinking. For now, it will remain simple as we only want to turn the state into frozen.

```java
public class FreezableFrozen implements Freezable {
    private AccountUnfrozen onUnfrozen;

    public FreezableFrozen(AccountUnfrozen onUnfrozen) {
        this.onUnfrozen = onUnfrozen;
    }

    @Override
    public Freezable deposit() {
        this.onUnfrozen.handle();
        return new FreezableActive();
    }

    @Override
    public Freezable withdraw() {
        this.onUnfrozen.handle();
        return new FreezableActive();
    }

    @Override
    public Freezable freezeAccount() {
        return this;
    }
}
```

This new class will be another implementation of the freezable interface. This is where that logic regarding account on freezing will move in. It will have to know about it the callback we used before, and it will effectively call it from the deposit and withdraw before telling the caller that the state has changed to active. The freeze account method, however, will have nothing to do because the account is already frozen. Even though the frozen state looks done, it has caused an ever in the active state in order to be able to advance the frozen state.

```
public class FreezableFrozen implements Freezable {
    private AccountUnfrozen onUnfrozen;

    public FreezableFrozen(AccountUnfrozen onUnfrozen) {
        this.onUnfrozen = onUnfrozen;
    }

    @Override
    public Freezable deposit() {
        return this.unfreeze();
    }

    @Override
    public Freezable withdraw() {
        return this.unfreeze();
    }

    private Freezable unfreeze() {
        this.onUnfrozen.handle();
        return new FreezableActive(this.onUnfrozen);
    }

    @Override
    public Freezable freezeAccount() {
        return this;
```

The active state also has to know about that
mandatory call back. This is unfortunate as
it inflates the code required to complete the
state pattern implementation to make the
full circle. I'll have to fix the location where
active state is in Stan, she ated. That was all.

```java
public class Account {
    private boolean isVerified;
    private boolean isClosed;
    private BigDecimal balance;
    private Freezable freezable;

    public Account(AccountUnfrozen onUnfrozen) {
        this.balance = BigDecimal.ZERO;
        this.freezable = new FreezableActive(onUnfrozen)
    }

    public void holderVerified() {
        this.isVerified = true;
    }

    public void closeAccount() {
        this.isClosed = true;
    }

    public void freezeAccount() {
        if (this.isClosed)
            return;   // Account must not be closed
        if (!this.isVerified)
            return; // Account must be verified first
        this.freezable = this.freezable.freezeAccount();
    }

    public void deposit(BigDecimal amount) {
        if (this.isClosed)
            return;   // Or do something more meaningful
        this.freezable = this.freezable.deposit();
        this.balance = this.balance.add(amount);
    }

    public void withdraw(BigDecimal amount) {
        if (!this.isVerified)
            return;   // Or do something more meaningful
        if (this.isClosed)
            return;
        this.freezable = this.freezable.withdraw();
        this.balance = this.balance.subtract(amount);
    }
}
```

Let's look at the consumer, the account past. What does all this mean to the account? This ensure and frozen object and the related own and frozen core back were the root cause, which has led us to invention of the free Zobel interface. Let's remove done. I don't want tohave to think about when the right moment is to act. The last two operations unfreeze and stay on frozen usedto be responsibility of the account class. Now they have Bean implemented in the freeze herbal classes. The only thing I do want to see as part of the account class is the freeze herbal object itself. Initially, the state will be active. You see how the new design nicely fits into the old design. Only note that I have to keep record of the new state that comes out from each people made of the freeze herbal element. This completes the part in which we're using the Freeze Herbal State Bottom line. If this moment is that we have achieved two important improvements in the account class, the first is removal off any explicit logic that deals with freezing. The entire logic was wrapped in separate classes. Another improvement is that all other stuff that have to do with freezing and unfreezing is now moved to those other classes. In particular, calling the injected behavior when the account is unfrozen is none of the accounts of business anymore. If you're not impressed with the results, stay with me for just a few minutes more and you will see all the rest of the account states starting to migrate out of this class, too.

Moving All State-related Functions into State Objects

What are the responsibilities of the account class now from its state, we can tell that the account is managing balance, but also managing, closing, verifying and freezing. Why not move? These responsibilities were freezable State is implemented. I can define even more states like closed or not verified, like frozen and active, which are there already, So, I will rename this interface from Freezable to AccountsState.

```
public interface AccountState {
    AccountState deposit();
    AccountState withdraw();
    AccountState freezeAccount();
    AccountState holderVerified();
    AccountState closeAccount();
}
```

```
v accountstates
    Active
    Closed
    Frozen
    NotVerified
Account
AccountState
AccountUnfrozen
EnsureUnfrozen
Main
```

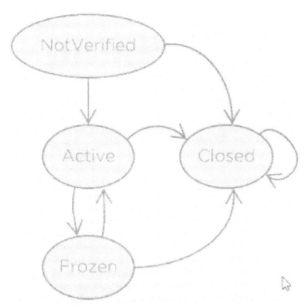

The other methods that used to affect state
will have to be added. Since more concrete
states are about to pop up, I will prepare a
nested package just for them. From now on,
this state will be known as active and this one
will be known as frozen. More states will
have to be added like not verified, which is
the initial state. When a new account is
created from this state, the account will moto
active or straight to closed. Let's define the
closed state. Then this completes the list of
concrete state classes. Now the
implementation We can start with a closed
state because it is already implemented.

```java
public class Closed implements AccountState {
    @Override
    public AccountState deposit() {
        return this;
    }

    @Override
    public AccountState withdraw() {
        return this;
    }

    @Override
    public AccountState freezeAccount() {
        return this;
    }

    @Override
    public AccountState holderVerified() {
        return this;
    }

    @Override
    public AccountState closeAccount() {
        return this;
    }
}
```

Whatever we try to do on a closed account, it will remain closed. It doesn't get much easier than this we can turn to the not verified state.

```java
public class NotVerified implements AccountState {
    @Override
    public AccountState deposit() {
        return this;
    }

    @Override
    public AccountState withdraw() {
        return this;
    }

    @Override
    public AccountState freezeAccount() {
        return this;
    }

    @Override
    public AccountState holderVerified() {
        return this;
    }

    @Override
    public AccountState closeAccount() {
        return new Closed();
    }
}
```

Then, when client asks the account to close itself, this state will turn into closed deposit method will be more engaged. Unlike close accounts, not verified ones will accept the deposits. The trouble is that the account cannot tell whether it accept or reject the deposit.

```
public void deposit(BigDecimal amount) {
    if (this.isClosed)
        return;    // Or do something more meani
    this.freezable = this.freezable.deposit();
    this.balance = this.balance.add(amount);
}
```

Above code in the box is not allowed in some states !

There is one technique which is not to use that often in modern programming callbacks. You will probably have a feeling that callbacks are so 19 eighties. Java has made callbacks looking younger for the concept off functional interfaces. Let me explain you the purpose of call back.

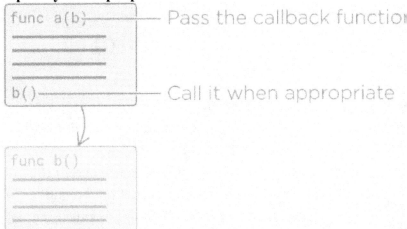

You may have to operations A and B and B operation must strictly execute after a How can we write the code that guarantees that one way is to pass be as a callback to A. Now a executes its body, whatever it is and then invokes be just before exiting. State knows whether the deposit should be accepted or not, but it doesn't know howto make it happen.

```
import java.math.BigDecimal;
import java.util.function.Consumer;

public interface AccountState {
    AccountState deposit(BigDecimal amount, Consumer<BigDecimal> addToBalance);
    AccountState withdraw();
    AccountState freezeAccount();
    AccountState holderVerified();
    AccountState closeAccount();
}
```

I will change the method signature and make it receive a money consumer. This object will be invoked when situation is right to. Add money to the balance now back to the not verified state

```
package com.accountstates;
import com.AccountState;
import com.AccountUnfrozen;
import java.math.BigDecimal;
import java.util.function.Consumer;
public class NotVerified implements AccountState {
    @Override
    public AccountState deposit(BigDecimal amount, Consumer<BigDecimal> addToBalance) {
        addToBalance.accept(amount);
        return this;
    }
    @Override
```

```java
    public AccountState withdraw() {
        return this;
    }
    @Override
    public AccountState freezeAccount() {
        return this;
    }
    @Override
    public AccountState holderVerified() {
        return this;
    }
    @Override
    public AccountState closeAccount() {
        return new Closed();
    }
}
```

deposit should be accepted in the not a verified state and account should remain not verified. This is how it goes. That is all you can see from this example how the code back pattern helps ensure the flow off operations.

```java
package com.accountstates;
import com.AccountState;
import java.math.BigDecimal;
import java.util.function.Consumer;
public class Closed implements AccountState
{
    @Override
```

```java
    public AccountState deposit(BigDecimal
amount, Consumer<BigDecimal>
addToBalance) {
        return this; // Ignores the callback
    }
    @Override
    public AccountState withdraw(BigDecimal
balance, BigDecimal amount,
                    Consumer<BigDecimal>
subtractFromBalance) {        return this;
    }
    @Override
    public AccountState freezeAccount() {
        return this;
    }
    @Override
    public AccountState holderVerified() {
        return this;
    }
    @Override
    public AccountState closeAccount() {
        return this;
    }
}
```

For example, in the closed state, this same callback would not be involved. The arguments are simply ignored.

```java
package com.accountstates;
import com.AccountState;
import com.AccountUnfrozen;
```

```java
import java.math.BigDecimal;
import java.util.function.Consumer;
public class NotVerified implements
AccountState {
  @Override
  public AccountState deposit(BigDecimal
amount, Consumer<BigDecimal>
addToBalance) {
    addToBalance.accept(amount);
    return this;
  }
  @Override
  public AccountState withdraw() {
    return this;
  }
  @Override
  public AccountState freezeAccount() {
    return this;
  }
  @Override
  public AccountState holderVerified() {
    return new Active();
  }
  @Override
  public AccountState closeAccount() {
    return new Closed();
  }
}
```

This time withdrawal will not be allowed on the non verified account, so it only remains non verified. Freezing will supposedly make no effect on non verified accounts, either. If customer wanted to change that, I would have to introduce a new state, something I frozen, not verified. And once the account holder is verified, the state will step to active.

```java
package com.accountstates;
import com.AccountState;
import com.AccountUnfrozen;
import java.math.BigDecimal;
import java.util.function.Consumer;
public class Active implements AccountState
{
    private AccountUnfrozen onUnfrozen;
    public Active(AccountUnfrozen
onUnfrozen) {
        this.onUnfrozen = onUnfrozen;
    }
    @Override
    public AccountState deposit(BigDecimal
amount, Consumer<BigDecimal>
addToBalance) {
        addToBalance.accept(amount);
        return this;
    }
    @Override
    public AccountState withdraw(BigDecimal
balance, BigDecimal amount,
                    Consumer<BigDecimal>
subtractFromBalance) {
        if (balance.compareTo(amount) >= 0) {
```

```java
        subtractFromBalance.accept(amount);
        }
        return this;
    }
    @Override
    public AccountState freezeAccount() {
        return new Frozen(this.onUnfrozen);
    }
    @Override
    public AccountState holderVerified() {
        return this;
    }
    @Override
    public AccountState closeAccount() {
        return new Closed();
    }
}
```

Now active constructor requires that the notification object, but I won't supply it yet our complete bodies of all methods and then unify them in one sweep. You will see that in a minute apart from this deficiency, not verified, state is complete. The active stated itself will be more engaged than other states. Every deposit will be accepted unconditionally, but withdrawal will now be more detailed. Taking more than the account contains will not be allowed, but the account itself will remain active unconditionally Holder verified and close account will be straightforward. The last state to implement is frozen.

```java
package com.accountstates;
import com.AccountState;
import com.AccountUnfrozen;
import java.math.BigDecimal;
import java.util.function.Consumer;
public class Frozen implements
AccountState {
  private AccountUnfrozen onUnfrozen;
  public Frozen(AccountUnfrozen
onUnfrozen) {
    this.onUnfrozen = onUnfrozen;
  }
  @Override
  public AccountState deposit(BigDecimal
amount, Consumer<BigDecimal>
addToBalance) {
    addToBalance.accept(amount);
    return this.unfreeze();
  }
  @Override
  public AccountState withdraw(BigDecimal
balance, BigDecimal amount,
                Consumer<BigDecimal>
subtractFromBalance) {
    if (balance.compareTo(amount) >= 0) {

subtractFromBalance.accept(amount);
    }
    return this.unfreeze();
```

```
    }
    private AccountState unfreeze() {
        this.onUnfrozen.handle();
        return new Active(this.onUnfrozen);
    }
    @Override
    public AccountState freezeAccount() {
        return this;
    }
    @Override
    public AccountState holderVerified() {
        return this;
    }
    @Override
    public AccountState closeAccount() {
        return new Closed();
    }
}
```

This implementation is a duplicate of that from the active state. If it got worse, I would probably opt for a base class shared between active and frozen states but replacing tree lines of duplicate code with two lines of unique code. Plus, the whole new class doesn't seem to pay the bill.

```
package com;
import java.math.BigDecimal;
import java.util.function.Consumer;
public interface AccountState {
```

```
    AccountState deposit(BigDecimal amount,
Consumer<BigDecimal> addToBalance);
    AccountState withdraw(BigDecimal
balance, BigDecimal amount,
                Consumer<BigDecimal>
subtractFromBalance);
    AccountState freezeAccount();
    AccountState holderVerified();
    AccountState closeAccount();
}
```

We don't know behavior implemented in states. I can walk for types and unify their constructors and the interfaces. The withdrawal method will accept money related arguments and all concrete states except closed. We'll have to keep track of the owner and frozen object because they can all eventually lead to the frozen state, which effectively uses this object. Finally, the account class remains to be cleaned up.

```
package com;
import com.accountstates.Active;
import java.math.BigDecimal;
public class Account {
    private BigDecimal balance;
    private AccountState state;
    public Account(AccountUnfrozen
onUnfrozen) {
        this.balance = BigDecimal.ZERO;
        this.state = new Active(onUnfrozen);
```

```java
    }
    public void holderVerified() {
        this.state = this.state.holderVerified();
    }
    public void closeAccount() {
        this.state = this.state.closeAccount();
    }
    public void freezeAccount() {
        this.state = this.state.freezeAccount();
    }
    public void deposit(BigDecimal amount) {
        this.state = this.state.deposit(amount,
this::addToBalance);
    }
    private void addToBalance(BigDecimal
amount) {
        this.balance =
this.balance.add(amount);
    }
    public void withdraw(BigDecimal amount)
{
        this.state = this.state.withdraw(
            this.balance, amount,
this::subtractFromBalance);
    }
    private void
subtractFromBalance(BigDecimal amount) {
        this.balance =
this.balance.subtract(amount);
    }
}
```

The hard part is behind us, and the rest will be smooth sailing for us. The remaining flags will disappear. Verifying the account holder or closing the account will now rely entirely on the state object, and so will the freezing. These tests have been replaced with a selection off a concrete stake, and now the true behavior comes in the deposit method. It will not verify the state, and it will not decide when and whether to increase the balance. That will be the decision of the concrete state, whichever it is in every call. Separately, we cannot tell whether the ads to balance method will be invoked, but we don't care to know either. The same transformation will happen to the withdrawal method. It is only responsible to specify how the balance is reduced in case that somebody needs that look at the class implementation. Now more than half of it is gone and all the branching instructions are gone. What remained is taking care of the balance, which makes sense the entire classes now unconditional. There's not a single if instruction here anymore. And all the logic in concrete states is also unconditional. Except in the with drome. Methods were execution that pants on the argument value which cannot be predicted and therefore must be compared to the balance to decide. The type of the state object is playing the role of the branching instruction. If we hold an object off one type, we will effectively invoke one method that run time. If we hold an object off another type, then another method will be involved. Everything is the same as Brandy, only with no explicit branching anymore. That is how we can leverage polymorphic method calls to substitute branching instructions.

Assessing Improvement

Now that the refactoring is complete, we can analyze what we have done.

Introducing Objects to the Design

Account
BigDecimal balance boolean isVerified boolean isClosed boolean isFrozen UnfreezeAction onUnfreeze
holderVerified() closeAccount() freezeAccount() deposit(amount) withdraw(amount)

The original implementation was object bays but not object oriented. Look at the class diagram one cars and that is all. All functionality was dumped into a single class that is not object oriented programming. And let's see the class diagram for the final solution.

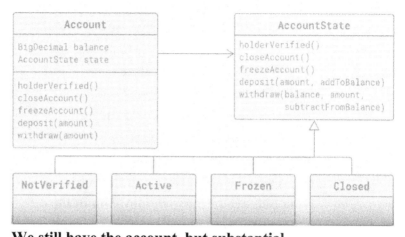

We still have the account, but substantial part of the domain logic has been moved out to smaller classes and replaced with the accounts state interface. This design is more object oriented, def for no other reason than because we finally have objects. But there are other riel benefits We have already analyzed testing aspect of the account class. There were total off 11 tests identified in the original implementation after only scratching the surface. After adding more scenarios, I came up with 26 tests, but I didn't show that in the demo. The problem is that even those 26 tests were not exhausted. I could have continued this time we don't care about concrete operations, but rather about interaction with a state object. Did each public method delegated the call to the state? Did it set the accounts staged to what that method has returned. Now repeat these two tests for each public method. Deposit withdrawal, close account, freeze account. Even if we added more states, a later number of tests for the account class would remain forever after the rest of the logic is distributed over smaller state classes, and each of them would be tested separately in isolation from all others. Did they not verified? State called the air to balance method with the correct argument. Did they not verified state skip to call the subtract from balance because money cannot be withdrawn from a non verified account? In the end, we would have a truly exhaustive set of pests for this system off very high quality and the usefulness enemy. This book is not about testing. I have just used the unit testing as an indication off a better design. Take one final look at the account class before we close this mantra. What is this class doing you now? It is only managing balance and nothing more. All other behavior was just delegated to a single object. It refers. The current state

Summary

A poorly designed class example :
- It tries to do everything by itself
- Relies on if-else instructions
- Behavior was factored out into other classes

In this module, we have seen an example of one class which was trying to do everything by itself. One of the issues with this class was that implementation off its methods was greatly based on the fells instructions. Applying the State design pattern :
- Hold a reference to the current state object
- Substitute the reference when state changes
In a couple of three factories that followed, you could see the process of moving operations in to. External states. Current state of the object was represented by current reference to a state object. If the state was to be changed as a result of some operation, the underlying reference to the state object with change.
Benefits from turning state into an object
- Class remains focused on primary role
- Other roles delegated to state objects
- Each state class also handles one role
Several benefits naturally come out from such approach. Class becomes simple and focused on its primary role. Secondary roles are delegated to, others each off those others by itself will become simple and focus on its own primary role. Thank you for watching this module. I hope that you have learned something new from this demo. In the next module, we will talk about immutable object and how they can be used to construct more stable and even simpler, object oriented

code. This was just the beginning, and there's a lot of code awaiting us

Module 4 : Using Immutable Objects and Value Objects

Causing a Bug that Comes from a Mutable State

Have you ever heard of the term aliasing bug? Have you ever been a victim off one of them? I will show you a couple of such backs and you will know as soon as you see them. Yes, We have all been victims off aliasing bugs many times. . In this module, we will talk about issues that come packaged together with mutable objects, objects that can change internal state after they have been constructed.

```
package com;
public class Demo {
    private void buy(Money wallet, Money
cost) {

    }
    public void run() {
```

```
    }
}

package com.codinghelmet.moreoojava;
import java.math.BigDecimal;
import java.math.RoundingMode;
public class Money implements
Comparable<Money> {
    private BigDecimal amount;
    private Currency currency;
    public Money(BigDecimal amount,
Currency currency) {
        this.amount = amount.setScale(2,
RoundingMode.HALF_UP);
        this.currency = currency;
    }
    public void scale(double factor) {
 this.amount = this.amount.multiply(new
BigDecimal(factor)).setScale(2,
RoundingMode.HALF_UP);
    }
    @Override
    public int compareTo(Money other) {
        return
this.compareAmountTo(this.currency.compa
reTo(other.currency), other);
    }
    private int compareAmountTo(int
currencyCompare, Money other) {
        return currencyCompare == 0 ?
this.amount.compareTo(other.amount)
```

```java
        : currencyCompare;
    }
    @Override
    public String toString() {
        return this.amount + " " +
this.currency;
    }
}
package com;
import java.math.BigDecimal;
public final class Currency implements
Comparable<Currency> {
    private String symbol;
    public Currency(String symbol) {
        this.symbol = symbol;
    }
    public Money zero() {
        return new Money(BigDecimal.ZERO,
this);
    }
    @Override
    public int compareTo(Currency other) {
        return
this.symbol.compareTo(other.symbol);
    }
    @Override
    public String toString() { return
this.symbol; }
}
```

Here is an empty dem across which I will use
to demonstrate one common mistake in

programming. Suppose that we are implementing some e commerce application. We would like to implement the selling feature. Let's start by adding a function named by this function will accept to arguments one indicating how much money the buyer has in the vault and the other indicating the cost of whatever we are selling. This money class will be there to wrap two concepts together amount of money and the currency. I'm not going to have a much larger than this class yet. I wanted money, objects Toby comparable and therefore the classes implementing the comparable off money interface to compare to monies. We compare their currencies and then they're amounts. Currency is also very simple. It only wraps around a string representing the currency symbol and it is also comparable. That is all it does. The only operation defined and money is this scale method. It can be used to scare the amount stored in this money object by a given factor. Back to the task of selling goods.

```java
package com;
import java.math.BigDecimal;
import java.util.HashMap;
import java.util.Map;
public class Demo {

    private void reserve(Money cost) {
```

```java
        System.out.println("Reserving an item
costing " + cost);
    }
    private void buy(Money wallet, Money
cost) {
        boolean enoughMoney =
wallet.compareTo(cost) >= 0;
        this.reserve(cost);
        if (enoughMoney)
            System.out.println("You will pay " +
cost + " with your " + wallet);
        else
            System.out.println("You cannot pay
" + cost + " with your " + wallet);
    }
    public void run() {
        Currency usd = new Currency("USD");
        Money usd12 = new Money(new
BigDecimal(12), usd);
        Money usd10 = new Money(new
BigDecimal(10), usd);
        Money usd7 = new Money(new
BigDecimal(7), usd);
        this.buy(usd12, usd10);
        System.out.println();
        this.buy(usd7, usd10);
    }
}
```

We want to reserve an item before selling it.
I'm not tracking actual goods in this
implementation because money is quite
sufficient for me to make a buck. Did I say

bag already? Now here's the part that I
wanted to show you. Customers request thes
to check whether the buyer has enough
money. Then we reserve goods. The funny
part is that we reserve the article no matter
whether the buyer has enough money right
now or not. Then comes the buying and
selling part. I would just print out what has
happened. Can you see that back in this
function? I'm just kidding. There's no back.
I can demonstrate that I will put my $12 into
buying something that costs $10. That should
pass well. In the second attempt, I will try to
buy the same item only carrying $7 with me
that time

```
"C:\Program Files\AdoptOpenJDK\jdk-8.0.202.08\bin\java.exe" ...
Reserving an item costing 10.00 USD
You will pay 10.00 USD with your 12.00 USD

Reserving an item costing 10.00 USD
You cannot pay 10.00 USD with your 7.00 USD

Process finished with exit code 0
```

Messages on the output confirmed my first
purchase and rejected the second attempt. In
both cases, the item was reserved.
Everything looks fine. So where is the bag
then? And as I said already, there is no back.
Everything is working perfectly. Only there
is a weak spot in this implementation. It is
assuming that the reserve method is not
going to change its argument. Suppose that
the reserve matter this part of some other
class possibly hidden behind an abstract
interface. What if we didn't have the reserve

methods implementation to read? Then suppose that one implementation of reserves starts playing tricks on us. My future self changes the body of the method.

```java
package com;
import java.math.BigDecimal;
import java.util.HashMap;
import java.util.Map;
public class Demo {
private boolean isHappyHour;

  private void reserve(Money cost) {
if(this.isHappyHour){
 cost.scale(0.5);
}
    System.out.println("Reserving an item costing " + cost);
  }
  private void buy(Money wallet, Money cost) {
    boolean enoughMoney =
wallet.compareTo(cost) >= 0;
    this.reserve(cost);
    if (enoughMoney)
      System.out.println("You will pay " + cost + " with your " + wallet);
    else
      System.out.println("You cannot pay " + cost + " with your " + wallet);
  }
  public void run() {
    Currency usd = new Currency("USD");
```

```java
        Money usd12 = new Money(new
BigDecimal(12), usd);
        Money usd10 = new Money(new
BigDecimal(10), usd);
        Money usd7 = new Money(new
BigDecimal(7), usd);
        this.buy(usd12, usd10);
        System.out.println();
        this.buy(usd7, usd10);
    System.out.println();
    this.isHappyHour = true;
    this.buy(usd7, usd10);
        }
}
```

For example, The new requirement might be to introduce a happy hour. I will indicate that with a boolean property you will forgive me the use of bolean in this demonstration. Please don't do things like this in your own code Now the reserve method might cut the price to half during the happy hour. Don't question my implementation or try to see how far the changes will reach. And here is how far reaching this happy our future is ours. Stubbornly try to by the same item with the same insufficient sum of money. Only this time I'll be lucky to pop up in the middle of a happy hour. Look what will happen now.

```
"C:\Program Files\AdoptOpenJDK\jdk-8.0.202.08\bin\java.exe" ..
Reserving an item costing 10.00 USD
You will pay 10.00 USD with your 12.00 USD

Reserving an item costing 10.00 USD
You cannot pay 10.00 USD with your 7.00 USD

Reserving an item costing 5.00 USD
You cannot pay 5.00 USD with your 7.00 USD

Process finished with exit code 0
```

The first and the second purchase attempt to look fine, but 1/3 1 is weird. The message says that I cannot pay $5 with my $7 that a strange now it definitely do have a bag.

Discovering the Aliasing Bug

The problem with this kind of defect is that we cannot point to any particular line of code, which is defective. Each function alone looks correct. That is how we come to the field off.

Discovering an Alias :
    private void reserve(**Money cost**) { // name #1

    }
    private void buy(Money wallet, **Money cost**) { // name #2

    }
pointing both name#1 and name#2 to an object

A racing Baggs alias means that there are two references to the same object. It is like when the same object can be found under two names. That is why this term areas has been used to define the situation, and then one object starts the foul play.

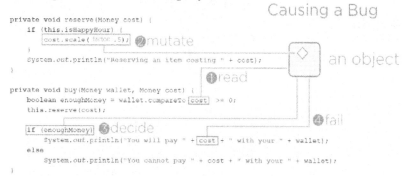

```
private void reserve(Money cost) {
    if (this.isHappyHour) {
        cost.scale( factor .5);
    }
    System.out.println("Reserving an item costing " + cost);
}

private void buy(Money wallet, Money cost) {
    boolean enoughMoney = wallet.compareTo cost >= 0;
    this.reserve(cost);

    if (enoughMoney)
        System.out.println("You will pay " + cost + " with your " + wallet);
    else
        System.out.println("You cannot pay " + cost + " with your " + wallet);
}
```

The first object reads the shared object. Then the second object writes the new content into it. Later, the first object continues doing things based on the earlier resumption. Unfortunately, the state of the share the object is now different. Another read would reveal that, but the object has run out of luck. It is not reading anything. It is already advancing in firm steps in the overall result will be incorrect. That is how alias ING bugs manifest. Basic technique to avoid them is to not the modify shared objects. A method argument is a good example of a shared reference.

```
private void reserve(Money cost) {
    if (this.isHappyHour) {
        cost.scale( factor .5);
    }
    System.out.println("Reserving an item costing " + cost);
}

private void buy(Money wallet, Money cost) {
    boolean enoughMoney = wallet.compareTo(cost) >= 0;
    this.reserve(cost);

    if (enoughMoney)
        System.out.println("You will pay " + cost + " with your " + wallet);
    else
        System.out.println("You cannot pay " + cost + " with your " + wallet);
}
```

an obje

The cost argument is a reference passed from the outside. The reserve method has every right to believe that somebody else is still keeping a valid reference to the same object.

```
private void reserve(Money cost) {
    if (this.isHappyHour) {
        cost.scale( factor .5);
    }
    System.out.println("Reserving an item costing " + cost);
}

private void buy(Money wallet, Money cost) {
    boolean enoughMoney = wallet.compareTo(cost) >= 0;
    this.reserve(cost);

    if (enoughMoney)
        System.out.println("You will pay " + cost + " with your " + wallet);
    else
        System.out.println("You cannot pay " + cost + " with your " + wallet);
}
```

an obje

And to avoid the risk, often a dressing bag, this method must refrain from modifying the argument. There is a slight ambiguity here. Having an alias doesn't mean that there is an alias in bag around. That is precisely the reason why a leasing box are so difficult to find in production code. There's nothing wrong with any part of the system, only

sometimes, and only if the system is assembled in some specific way. Those seemingly correct parts will not work together as expected. Therefore, one certain way to avoid a leasing box is to avoid ambiguity. If there is a chance that the reference we're holding is an alias, then refrain from modifying the object in that respect. This change we're making to the amount property of the cost object will not be allowed anymore. Modifying a price means to create a new modified money object. But how shall I do that when the original cost doesn't expose any means to construct another object from it? It's state is encapsulated. I cannot construct half of this amount because the cooler doesn't know the amount in the first place. One way to solve the problem is to lower the criteria and exposed state to the consumers. Luckily, this awful practice is not the only possibility.

```java
package com;
import java.math.BigDecimal;
import java.math.RoundingMode;
public class Money implements
Comparable<Money> {
    private BigDecimal amount;
    private Currency currency;
    public Money(BigDecimal amount,
Currency currency) {
```

```java
        this.amount = amount.setScale(2,
RoundingMode.HALF_UP);
        this.currency = currency;
    }
    public Money scale(double factor) {
        return new
Money(this.amount.multiply(new
BigDecimal(factor)), this.currency);
    }
    @Override
    public int compareTo(Money other) {
        return
this.compareAmountTo(this.currency.compa
reTo(other.currency), other);
    }
    private int compareAmountTo(int
currencyCompare, Money other) {
        return currencyCompare == 0 ?
this.amount.compareTo(other.amount)
        : currencyCompare;
    }
    @Override
    public String toString() {
        return this.amount + " " +
this.currency;
    }
}
```

We can also make the mutating method itself
constructed a new object to using the private
state. So we would basically keep the entire
state private and use it internally to

construct a modified object. This is proper
object or into the code. The mutating scale
method is constructing a brand new money
object with the scale, amount and the same
currency. The method must return the new
object so that the consumer can use it. We
have retained full state encapsulation and
dismissed any racing bag on the money
object in the future.

```java
public class Demo {
    private boolean isHappyHour;

    private void reserve(Money cost) {
        Money finalCost = this.isHappyHour ? cost.scale(.5) : cost;
        System.out.println("Reserving an item costing " + finalCost);
    }
}
```

At a consuming end, the final cost will either
be the scared cost or the original one. Based
on whether it is a happy hour or not. Forgive
me once again the use of branching in this
implementation. I didn't want to complicate
a demonstration by adding more classes.
This has brought us to the reserve matter
which does not affect its consumer to buy
method, and that is a good thing.

```
Main

"C:\Program Files\AdoptOpenJDK\jdk-8.0.202.08\bin\java.exe" ...
Reserving an item costing 10.00 USD
You will pay 10.00 USD with your 12.00 USD

Reserving an item costing 10.00 USD
You cannot pay 10.00 USD with your 7.00 USD

Reserving an item costing 5.00 USD
You cannot pay 10.00 USD with your 7.00 USD

Process finished with exit code 0
```

The only problem is that the buy method has no clue that the price has changed. The price was cut to half, but a dying still operates on full price. The back has moved to a different location. This situation looks no different than what we had before. Almost there is the Sutter change.

```java
package com;
import java.math.BigDecimal;
import java.util.HashMap;
import java.util.Map;
public class Demo {
    private boolean isHappyHour;
    private Money reserve(Money cost) {
        Money finalCost = this.isHappyHour ?
cost.scale(.5) : cost;
        System.out.println("Reserving an item
costing " + finalCost);
        return finalCost;
    }
    private void buy(Money wallet, Money
cost) {
        boolean enoughMoney =
wallet.compareTo(cost) >= 0;
        Money finalCost = this.reserve(cost);
        boolean finalEnough =
wallet.compareTo(finalCost) >= 0;
        if (finalEnough && !enoughMoney)
            System.out.println("Only this time,
you will pay " + finalCost + " with your " +
wallet);
        else if (finalEnough)
```

```
        System.out.println("You will pay " +
finalCost + " with your " + wallet);
      else
        System.out.println("You cannot pay
" + finalCost + " with your " + wallet);
    }
    public void run() {
      Currency usd = new Currency("USD");
      Money usd12 = new Money(new
BigDecimal(12), usd);
      Money usd10 = new Money(new
BigDecimal(10), usd);
      Money usd7 = new Money(new
BigDecimal(7), usd);
      this.buy(usd12, usd10);
      System.out.println();
      this.buy(usd7, usd10);
    System.out.println();
    this.isHappyHour = true;
    this.buy(usd7, usd10);
    }
}
```

For one thing, the result matter is not complete. It must also return the modified price. A method should not mutate its arguments. That would be a risky habit. We have seen it leading to an area Sing buck By returning the new value, the matter is telling that it might modify the input value. And then the ball is in the by methods court. It is damping the methods return to the garbage collector. Some compilers rise a warning. If you get your return from a method, this code shows why right here? Ignoring the return was the back. This was the missing part. And now the editor is rendering this value night color to indicate that its value was never used. Which helps me finally understand that I do have a bug I can finally think of completing all the possible scenarios there might have bean just enough money after the reserve method, or there might have been enough money all the time or the funds might have bean insufficient. Those are all the cases, some off, which I didn't cover because they were not clear that was the alias ing bug. In fact, the third, the demo is now working correctly. It has affected that purchase can be performed after the price was reduced.

Inventing the Value Objects

After this inter doctor example, we're ready to dig deeper and ask what the difference between primitive values and objects is.

```java
public void run() {
    Currency usd = new Currency( symbol: "USD");
    Money usd12 = new Money(new BigDecimal( val: 12), usd);
    Money usd10 = new Money(new BigDecimal( val: 10), usd);
    Money usd7 = new Money(new BigDecimal( val: 7), usd);

    this.buy(usd12, usd10);

    System.out.println();
    this.buy(usd7, usd10);

    System.out.println();
    this.isHappyHour = true;
    this.buy(usd7, usd10);

    System.out.println();
    int sum1 = 2 + 3;
}
}
```

How many objects are there in this line of code? Let's name them. Number two is one object number. Free is the second object. Number five well appear is the result of the summation operator that is the third object stored into sum1 variable. Could we do the same with money objects?

```
public void run() {
    Currency usd = new Currency( symbol: "USD");
    Money usd12 = new Money(new BigDecimal( val: 12), us
    Money usd10 = new Money(new BigDecimal( val: 10), us
    Money usd7 = new Money(new BigDecimal( val: 7), usd)

    this.buy(usd12, usd10);

    System.out.println();
    this.buy(usd7, usd10);

    System.out.println();
    this.isHappyHour = true;
    this.buy(usd7, usd10);

    System.out.println();
    int sum1 = 2 + 3;

    Money usd2 = new Money(new BigDecimal( val: 2), usd)
    Money usd3 = new Money(new BigDecimal( val: 3), usd)

    Money sum2 = usd2.add(usd3);
}
}
```

There is the object of \$2 in the objects off \$3.

package com;
import java.math.BigDecimal;
import java.math.RoundingMode;
public class Money implements
Comparable<Money> {
   private BigDecimal amount;
   private Currency currency;
   public Money(BigDecimal amount,
Currency currency) {
      this.amount = amount.setScale(2,
RoundingMode.HALF_UP);
      this.currency = currency;
   }

```
    public Money scale(double factor) {
        return new
Money(this.amount.multiply(new
BigDecimal(factor)), this.currency);
    }
    public Money add(Money other) {
        if
(other.currency.compareTo(this.currency) !=
0)
            throw new
IllegalArgumentException();
        return new
Money(this.amount.add(other.amount),
this.currency);
    }
//remaining methods
}
```

I have defined this ad method on the money
class, similar to the scare method, adding is
only defined on money's of the same
currency. The new money object is
constructed holding amount, which is the
sum of the two amounts and the same
currency is both objects involved. Then,
adding to money, objects together lead still
construction of the third object to which this
variable some too, will refer. Is there any
reason not to see money as a simple value,
like the birthday Nen teacher type?
Honestly, no, there is no reason to see these
two concepts as any different. This had the

lads to the invention off value objects, an important building block in object oriented programming.

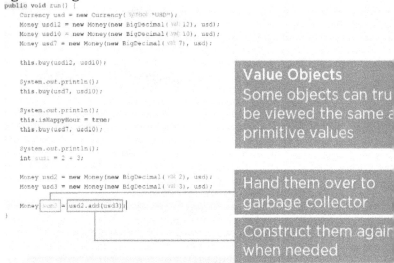

```
public void run() {

    Currency usd = new Currency( Symbol "USD");
    Money usd12 = new Money(new BigDecimal( val 12), usd);
    Money usd10 = new Money(new BigDecimal( val 10), usd);
    Money usd7 = new Money(new BigDecimal( val 7), usd);

    this.buy(usd12, usd10);

    System.out.println();
    this.buy(usd7, usd10);

    System.out.println();
    this.isHappyHour = true;
    this.buy(usd7, usd10);

    System.out.println();
    int sum = 2 + 3;

    Money usd2 = new Money(new BigDecimal( val 2), usd);
    Money usd3 = new Money(new BigDecimal( val 3), usd);

    Money sum3 = usd2.add(usd3);
}
```

Value Objects
Some objects can tru be viewed the same a primitive values

Hand them over to garbage collector

Construct them again when needed

Some objects are unchangeable overtime to such extreme that we can view than the same way with you primitive values. What is meant by that is that we can let the garbage collector destroy a money object. This $5 objects, for example, because we can construct another $5 money object at a later time, and nobody will ever know the difference. That is how value objects that became they're timeless. Constance, representing simple business elements, opposed the values we find entities.

```
public interface Painter {
    int getId();
    boolean isAvailable();
    Duration estimateTimeToPaint(double sqMeters);
    Money estimateCompensation(double sqMeters);
    String getName();
    double estimateSqMeters(Duration time);
}
```

An entity has a history of its own taken interface representing a painter, a person who paints wars. It's represents a really human being. We may enter a person into our register our database and keep track of them over time. The principal method of keeping track over time is through a signing up resistant identity to such an object. Identity helps us reconstruct an entity object much later in a different running off the application on a different computer if need be. Entities have their history. They have a time line over which they were changing, and we can track those changes as a matter of our business. Very objects on the other hand, are simple values that can be thrown away and reconstructed at will. And the fact that we do not track changes on values gives rise to the most important aspect of values. They are immutable, deeply mutable, mind you. Not only that, the money object doesn't change itself, but it only consists off value objects. This currency object is also immutable and big decimal library class is immutable as well. When developing a complex object model, you will recognize many value objects, objects that have all the qualities of planing teachers only that they are reference types instances of classes. In this , you will learn how you can model those glasses, is proper value objects and reap the benefits of their simplicity.

Turning Immutable Objects into Value Objects

We have started from preventing box and turned the objects immutable, which has led us to the invention off a value objects but in mutability is just 1/2 of the story. Been talking about values unless, sir, how Value objects also have the specific equality. Semantic values can be compared for equality for primitive types. Java provides the double equal operator, which returns true. If two values are equal, it doesn't work that way With classes dough Here, you can see that five is truly equal to five, but $5 are somehow not equal to other $5. The problem is that equal, equal operator doesn't implemented the value Tapped equality semantic in job. But this operator is testing reference equality. Two variables were the equal only if they refer to the same object. Otherwise, they're considered different even if objects they reference have the same content that finally brings the value tactic quality semantic to the table to value. Objects are equal if they're contained, objects are equal. That is all too money. Objects are equally. If they're amounts are equal and their currencies are equal. The definition is recursive, which means that contained objects must also be equal in depth in Java Value tactic qualities imagined to be performed using the equals method. Every class inherits the equals method from its ultimate abase class object. This matter cannot be involved on primitive types. In cases when you have to come up with a unified design, you can box a primitive value and call equals on its wrapper. I have boxed the someone variable into an in theater object, while Constant five will be out of boxed by the comm pyre. The equals method will then execute on two objects of class in teacher rather than on to primitive. Indeed, your number Alice. This won't work either. While the interior class has correctly concluded that two objects are equal, my custom money class has failed. That is because bays implementation inherited from the object is just a fallback, which compares references to provide true value tactic quality testing. In a custom class, you will have to override the equals matter and implement custom stayed comparison yourself and there comes the rule. Since value objects have no identity, their whole content is their identity to value. Objects are equal. If they're content is equal, you will always implemented the equals method by testing whether the objects components are equal.

```
@Override
public boolean equals(Object other) {
    return other instanceof Money && this.equals((Money)other);
}

private boolean equals(Money other) {
    return this.amount.equals(other.amount) && this.currency.equals(other.curren
}
```

For one thing we have, they're sure that the other references a known al object off type money. Be careful to dismiss corner cases First, we don't have to include the not check because instance off operator already evaluates the force. If other is now, then we can finally compare components. This implementation, however simple, is opening several subtitle issues. The simple problem is that components must also implement value typed equality. Semantic the big decimal class. The amount object here is already implementing it. There is a library class and it already comes with custom equals implementation.

package com;
import java.math.BigDecimal;
public final class Currency implements Comparable<Currency> {
    private String symbol;
    @Override
    public boolean equals(Object other) {

```
      return other instanceof Currency &&
this.equals((Currency)other);
   }
   private boolean equals(Currency other) {
      return
this.symbol.equals(other.symbol);
   }
   public Currency(String symbol) {
      this.symbol = symbol;
   }
   public Money zero() {
      return new Money(BigDecimal.ZERO,
this);
   }
   @Override
   public int compareTo(Currency other) {
      return
this.symbol.compareTo(other.symbol);
   }
   @Override
   public String toString() { return
this.symbol; }
}
```

On the other hand, this currency classes my custom type and it will have to come up with a proper equal solver ride. I'm repeating that same ritual again, testing the type and then comparing the only component the currency symbol. Both of the money and the currency classes have a subtle bag right now. Take this implementation the grain of salt because it is not entirely correct. Yet it will serve the purpose of this simple demo Before we get back to it to be the vengeance, there is more than my nation is short coat segment and I will have to solve them before this module ends. This time. $5 Object says that it is equal to another $5 object, just like the two in theaters with the same value are equal. In this demonstration, you have learned that value objects must implement value tactic quality semantic besides being immutable. But there is a catch and we are about to uncover a defect in current implementation that will lead us to the true way of implementing this same feature.

Completing the Value-typed Equality

```
@Override
public boolean equals(Object other)
```
The Equivalence Relation
  Reflexive: $a = a$
Symmetric: $a = b \Rightarrow b = a$
  Transitive: $a = b$ and $b = c \Rightarrow a = c$

```
@Override
public int compareTo(Money other)
```
The Total Order Relation
Antisymmetric: $a \leq b$ and $b \leq a \Rightarrow a = b$
      Transitive: $a \leq b$ and $b \leq c \Rightarrow a \leq c$
      Connexive: $a \leq b$ or $b \leq a$

Consistency Rule for
equals() and compareTo(

when a.compareTo(b) =
then a.equals(b) = tru

The equals method is supposed to implement the equivalents relation in mathematics. Equivalence is the binary relation between objects, which is reflexive, symmetric and transitive. You might wonder why anyone would insist on mathematical properties off a

88

method. The reason is simpler than you think. Consistency mathematical theory brings consistency to our code. For instance, compared to is implementing the relation of total order over the set off all money objects. Another mathematical relation total means that we can compare any two objects of this type. Equivalence is also a total relation. Jealous specification correctly mandates that equals and compared to should behave consistently. That means that zero returned from compared to implies, true returned from equals and vice versa. So the property's off equivalence reflex. Everything means that an object is equal to itself. Some people at an explicit reference comparison to make equals faster. This could be viewed as an explicit reflectivity guarantee. An object will always claim that it is equal to itself. I don't include this test in my designs because I have never noticed equals called on the same object too many times. That may be the result of my coding style is on a keen to reuse any objects at runtime. This test will probably make my equal slower. The next requested property is symmetry to objects must return the same result from their equals methods symmetry analysis will be more engaged, so I will leave it for the end Spoiler warning That is precisely where the bug is hiding in my implementation the third requested properties transitive ity. I'm testing equivalents off amounts and currencies and these two are already positive. Big decimus equals math of these transitive and currency is relying on strings implementation of equals which is also transitive Conjunction of two transitive relations is also transitive. We can easily proved that as a theorem life is easy when you have a consistent theory by your side. So my implementation is transitive anyway

```
@Override
public boolean equals(Object other) {
    return other instanceof Money && this.equals((Money)other);
}
```

```
baseObj    instanceof BaseType    = true
derivedObj instanceof BaseType    = true
baseObj    instanceof DerivedType = false
```

```
@Override
public int compareTo(Money other) {
    return this.compareAmountTo(this.currency.compareTo(other.currency), other)
}

private int compareAmountTo(int currencyCompare, Money other) {
    return currencyCompare == 0 ? this.amount.compareTo(other.amount)
        : currencyCompare;
}
```

Symmetry, symmetry E is where the problems are lurking in my design and I tell it frankly, it is broken. The instance off operator is reflexive. It is transitive, but it is not symmetric. It will evaluate to true when applied to an object off a derived class too. But it won't work the other way around. This object, which is of type of money, will make instance offer valued to false in the derived class, that is where symmetry will break down. If you think that this analysis is overly abstracted, that I'm strangling you with dry theory which doesn't apply the rial

programming. Then let me quote an old saying, If it doesn't work on paper, it ain't gonna work in code either.

```java
public class Euro extends Money {
    private String iso2Country;

    public Euro(BigDecimal amount, Currency currency, String iso2Country) {
        super(amount, currency);
        this.iso2Country = iso2Country;
    }

    @Override
    public boolean equals(Object other) {
        return other instanceof Euro && this.equals((Euro)other);
    }

    private boolean equals(Euro other) {
        return super.equals(other) && this.iso2Country.equals(other.iso2Country);
    }

    @Override
    public String toString() {
        return super.toString() + " (" + this.iso2Country + ")";
    }
}
```

Here you have it. Ah, Bug. You may know that countries in the European Union are using euro as their currency. You may also known that the euro's air printed in every country that uses them with slight differences. Hence, my financial model keeps track of the money's country off origin to euro class extends money. It lets the base class keep amount and currency while storing the country code in its own state. It's equals repeats the same medium. Only the base state equality test is now delegated to the base class while country code is tested here. This model works well with the vending machines. For example, they're

usually fine tuned to accept coins minted in
the country where the machine is in store.
Attempting to insert a coin from a different
European country would probably not work
because it's wait differs from what was
expected by the control mechanism. So we
have the proper object model, which fits the
reality. Let's try to use it here.

```
Currency eur = new Currency( symbol "EUR");
Money eur2 = new Money(new BigDecimal( val 2), eur);
Euro coin = new Euro(new BigDecimal( val 2), eur, iso2Country "de");

System.out.println();
System.out.println(eur2 + " is " + (eur2.equals(coin) ? "" : "not ") + "equal to " + co
System.out.println(coin + " is " + (coin.equals(eur2) ? "" : "not ") + "equal to " + eu
```

I have two euros in money, which it doesn't
care to know its country of origin. And I
have a two euros coin minted in Germany.
How did they compare for equality?

```
Main
"C:\Program Files\AdoptOpenJDK\jdk-8.0.202.08\bin\java.exe"
Reserving an item costing 10.00 USD
You will pay 10.00 USD with your 12.00 USD

Reserving an item costing 10.00 USD
You cannot pay 10.00 USD with your 7.00 USD

Reserving an item costing 5.00 USD
Only this time, you will pay 5.00 USD with your 7.00 USD

5 is equal to 5
5.00 USD is equal to 5.00 USD

2.00 EUR is equal to 2.00 EUR (de)
2.00 EUR (de) is not equal to 2.00 EUR

Process finished with exit code 0
```

I wonder. I will ask them to compare with
each other both ways and there we encounter
an issue based object claims it is equal to the

derived object. But a derived object knows it better, and it says that they are not the equal. The symmetry property of the equivalence relation is broken.

```java
public class Euro extends Money {
    private String iso2Country;

    public Euro(BigDecimal amount, Currency currency, String iso2Country) {
        super(amount, currency);
        this.iso2Country = iso2Country;
    }

    @Override
    public boolean equals(Object other) {
        return other instanceof Euro && this.equals((Euro)other);
    }

    private boolean equals(Euro other) {
        return super.equals(other) && this.iso2Country.equals(other.iso2Country);
    }

    @Override
    public String toString() {
        return super.toString() + " (" + this.iso2Country + ")";
    }
}
```

Here is the problem. Euro dismisses the money object because it cannot perform the detailed comparison. But money is happy to compare itself with euro. It would effectively ignored the additional state and only compare the bass parts of the two objects. Since both have the same amount in the same currency, money considers them equal. That problem is due to sub typing, interface, implementation or class inheritance. All the same objects of different types cannot be safely compared for equality. They must be considered unequal. Now that we understand the problem. Let's fix the bug. The easiest way to ensure equivalent symmetry Usedto forbid sub typing whenever possible. Model value objects is final classes. There will never be a different kind of a currency in my model. T equals implementation based on the instance off operator will then be correct. It won't go so easy with the money class. Sometimes not too often, though, you will encounter a value object which exhibits the need for some passing. Don't this Bayer? Remember, the principal objects of different types are different.

```
@Override
public boolean equals(Object other) {
    return other != null && other.getClass() == this.getClass() && this.equals((Money)ot
}
```

An object must be known no, and it's type must exactly match the type of the current object. Class objects are reused so you can safely compared them by reference. This has fixed the base implementation, often extendable class. Now the same protocol must be repeated in all the right glasses. Notes. The time doing this only because of derived class had state with no added state. The only difference would be an object types, and that difference is already handled by the inherited equals method. Hence, you will override equals in the derived class only if it adds state, which has to be compared for equality. This has fixed the problem and equivalents implementation is finally symmetric. Both objects now claim that they're not equal to each other.

Using Value Objects as Keys

The last demonstration in this module will relate to using value objects as keys. We can use primitive values as keys to an indexing collection. We have to box, the primitive valued Oh, it is truly annoying to see that the Java generics do not apply to primitive types. Anyway, I'm sure that I will find the meaning oflife by the T 42. But what if I tried to use my custom value object money as the key? The new code is structured the same. Only this time I'm using $42 in a desperate search for the meaning oflife minded that I am constructing a new money object when creating the cash map by using two distinct references, I want to dismiss any accidental results. Will I be lucky this time? No sorry. Associating items within teachers works fine, but using money as the key has failed, the search has failed even though the equal money object was inserted into the map only one line of code earlier. I'm still keen to construct a custom class which behaves is a true value where any other value, with the same content matches the pry value in all execution scenarios. While napping is one common executioner scenario but in which custom equals method is not the only requirement. Mapping in Java comes in two guys, is the simple one is based on repeatedly testing objects for equality like when traversing a listing comparing objects. The other form of mapping is much more powerful, and it is based on the hashing principle. Every value object should calculate an interior value called the cash value or hash code. This value must be calculated from the same values that are used in the equals. Implementation has two objects with the same content would produce the same hash value. Also, the hash value for an object must be stable. It must not change during the lifetime of an object, and another note. The in theater types range is limited and hands some distinct objects will eventually collide. However, dashing function should be smart enough to disperse. The objects over the in teacher types range as uniformly as realistically possible. Then the mapping structures come to the table. Hash map is the typical example here. They use the hash code, often object to find the right place inside the data structure. When another object comes, the structure doesn't ask. It's to compare to the first object. Instead, it asks it for its hash code. Only then the structure might encounter the previous object indexed under the same hash code, and only then will the structure called the equals method to compare them. The myriads off other objects in the data structure will be spared from having to execute their costly equals matters. Now comes the understanding of properties of cashing function should comply with it must be stable. If an object was indexed under one hash code, it must not change its mind later because the data structure has already made its mind about the objects. Position cashing function to this purse objects evenly. If many objects map to the same hash code than equals, method will be called many times, and performance benefits of cashing will be lost. That is the hashing principle, one of the most important principles in data structures. It leads to invention off exceptionally performance collections such as the hash map. Anyway, for a value objects to be useful in a cashing structure, it must produce the cash code. Every class inherits the cash code method from object that is the place where you would implement your own cashing function tailored to your custom type. Since his code is the consequence of objects content, you'd usually combined cash codes of contained objects. Multiplying by some small prime number is a common strategy. A somewhat faster but not so good. Combinator is the ex orbit wise operator. You should look for functions that are dispersing the values batter, so the multiplying auction is a better choice. Anyway, this moves focused. The components cash code must be implemented in death. Big Decimal comes with a good hash code function of its own. On the other hand, currency is my custom type, and it will have to come up with its own hash code. Lucky for me, the string class comes with an exceptionally good hash code implementation. I'm more than happy to delegate the call to the string component. The last class in my model is the specialized euro class. It will rely on base hash code and then add its own flavor to the result that complete support for hashing in my custom value objects. Implementing hash code is mandatory whenever custom Equus is implemented. In my opinion, compiler should break the build if equal sees over ridden without a corresponding override off cash code one without the other is a bug which will manifest the first time someone tries to use. Your class is a key to a data structure based on cashing. If I run the application now, you will witness the two distinct money objects have been matched. It is so because the cash map has received the same hash code from both objects, and then it has located the one inside the structure called It's Equals Method and conclusively found the value associated with that key.

Summary

Immutable objects and values
- Immutability is simple to implement
- Saves us from bugs
- Rules out aliasing bugs
In this module, we have touched the sore point of many object oriented applications. The question off immutable objects and values. We have seen how easy it is to introduce the mutability to certain classes. We have seen that the mutability where applicable can save us from making box that are hard to discover. Namely, the alias ING box can hit mutable objects. The mutability is ruling out alias in bags by its definition.
Immutable objects can behave as values
- Value objects behave as plain values
- No different than int or a string
- Makes code easy to maintain
After that, we have seen that we can make another big leap forward. Immutable objects can be turned into proper value objects value objects can be used with the same semantic explain values such a Zen teacher numbers or strings. With some investment in class design and implementation value, semantic brings huge revenues back in maintain ability and application stability.
Implementing value-typed semantic
- Value objects must be immutable

- They must override the equals method
- equals is reflexive, symmetric, transitive
- They must override hashCode
- Hash code must be stable and uniform

In this module, you have learned that value objects must be mutable. They must implement equals method, which is reflexive, symmetric and transit E, and they must implement the hash code method, which is stable and disperses objects over the interior range.

Pitfalls of equivalence
- equals implements equivalence relation
- Base and derived objects are not equivalent
- Otherwise, they would violate symmetry
- Objects of the same type are equal if their components are equal
- Value object only consists of values

You have seen the pitfalls of equality. The equals method implements the equivalence. Mathematical relation, equivalence, off base and derived objects must be prohibited because it violates the symmetry property it remains. The two objects of the same type will be equal if their components are equal. Value objects, therefore, can only consist off other value objects. In the next module, we will turn to another sore point in object oriented programming. Now references. We will start investigating techniques that are making it possible to write the Java code without ever assigning now to a reference.

Module 5 : Leveraging Special Case Objects to Remove Null Checks

Understanding the Problem of Null

How many times did you have to test whether our variable in your hands is now before proceeding? Wouldn't it be great if now never existed? In this module, we will tackle one of the most prominent sources of complexity, but also the great source of defects in code null references.

```
public interface Warranty {
    boolean isValidOn(LocalDate date);
}
```

This is the warranty interface it models. Warrant is issued when goods are sold. The E is valid. Own method tests whether the warranty is valid on a given day.

```
package com;
public class Article {
    private Warranty moneyBackGuarantee;
    private Warranty expressWarranty;
```

```java
    private Article(Warranty
moneyBackGuarantee, Warranty
expressWarranty) {
    this.moneyBackGuarantee =
moneyBackGuarantee;
    this.expressWarranty =
expressWarranty;
  }
  public Warranty
getMoneyBackGuarantee() { return
moneyBackGuarantee; }
  public Warranty getExpressWarranty() {
return expressWarranty; }
}
```

Then we model. The article sold to a customer it exposes to warrant is money back guarantee and the express warranty we can attach to warranty objects to every article. We can even pres ist the object with those warranties attached, of course, later, a customer might return with broken stuff. We sold them with a fancy idea of claiming warranty. Let's try to write a function for that requirement.

```java
public class Demo {
  public void claimWarranty(Article article,
boolean isInGoodCondition, boolean
isNonOperational) {
    LocalDate today = LocalDate.now();
  if(isInGoodCondition && isNonOperational
&&
```

```java
article.getMoneyBackGuarantee() != null
&&
article.getMoneyBackGuarantee().isValidO
n(today)){
 System.out.println("Offer money back");
 }
 if(isNonOperational &&
article.getExpressWarranty() != null &&
article.getExpressWarranty().isValidOn(tod
ay)){
 System.out.println("Offer repair");
 }
    System.out.println("----------------");
  }
  public void run() {

  }
}
```

This is the date on which the complaint has been filed. Since there are two kinds off warranties, we could offer both or one or none of them, depending on conditions for example, money returned might be offered. If article is in good condition and not operational, I will use boolean flags to make things worse. There's no other reason for billions. Honestly, One of the principal signs that you're doing something wrong is accumulation off method arguments. We will inevitably return to this issue later. Pre arguments, two of them born Ian is a symptom that I have already left object oriented programming in favor of something that is not the object oriented in object oriented programming. You tell objects what to do and they choose how to do it. With these flags in place, I'm ready to start thinking howto warrant his apply to an Arctic, and that is a bad idea. Already. The rules are if article looks good, doesn't work and the money back guarantee has not expired. Then we offer money back, not related to money back. If the item is defunct and express warrant is in effect, we offer a repair. Does this implementation sound reasonable to you? Maybe. But look, I have already ignored the possibility that one or both warranties were set to another reference. I have to guard against the null in both cases. In my opinion, this implementation is too complicated. Branching over boolean flags and now checks is a poor programming practice, and it has nothing in common with object oriented programming. Null references are especially dangerous because if we forget to put a guard the subsequent attempt, to the reference, the variable will fail with the null pointer exception in this module, we will apply what we have learned during the book to remove all flags and the null references so that we don't have to worry whether our logic is safe. And here is one option.

```
public class Demo {
```

```java
    public void claimWarranty(Article article)
{
    LocalDate today = LocalDate.now();
    if(article.getMoneyBackGuarantee().isValid
On(today)){
  System.out.println("Offer money back");
  }

    if(article.getExpressWarranty().isValidOn(to
day)){
  System.out.println("Offer repair");
  }
    System.out.println("----------------");
  }
    public void run() {

  }
}
```

For one thing, I want all boolean conditions
to be removed. If you were to only remember
one sentence from this book, then it should
be this one. Don't branch around boolean
flags and the new house. If you were to
remember another one, then that would be
don't possible in flag, says method
arguments. I only need to know if the
warranty is valid on this day. Everything else
is somebody else's responsibility in real life,
the clerk receiving warranty claims with
check the article, but in programming it
doesn't necessarily go that way. Welcome to
the ram off objects who is responsible to

know whether the article is in good condition. The article, you know, object oriented programming objects are responsible to know their conditions with a drop off. Magic disclaim warranting method will then become significantly simpler. So the request will be that the article object knows its condition and operability and it never returns. Now from methods returning warranties in this module, I will assure you how we can satisfy those requests. And once we do, that code will suddenly become simpler. Even these last two branching instructions will go away.

Introducing Null Objects

This glass article is now facing a sharp requirement. His consumers don't expect enough from its getters. It is always a good idea to get into the caller's shoes. What is the caller's situation here? The caller gets the warranty and asks if it is valid. When you see a call like this, you assume that you will get the object now is not then object. So this getter is effectively promising to return Unknown al result. The fact that so many programmers return and now from a get the method only means that they are playing tricks and nothing more. Now the article is

forwarding that pressure to whoever has in Stan. She ate it.

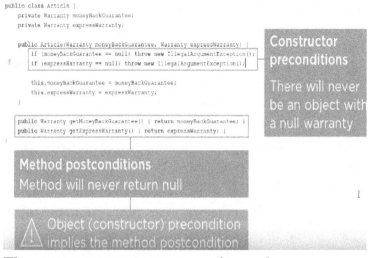

```
public class Article {

    private Warranty moneyBackGuarantee;
    private Warranty expressWarranty;

    public Article(Warranty moneyBackGuarantee, Warranty expressWarranty) {
        if (moneyBackGuarantee == null) throw new IllegalArgumentException();
        if (expressWarranty == null) throw new IllegalArgumentException();

        this.moneyBackGuarantee = moneyBackGuarantee;
        this.expressWarranty = expressWarranty;
    }

    public Warranty getMoneyBackGuarantee() { return moneyBackGuarantee; }
    public Warranty getExpressWarranty() { return expressWarranty; }
}
```

Constructor preconditions

There will never be an object with a null warranty

Method postconditions
Method will never return null

Object (constructor) precondition implies the method postcondition

The constructor must never receive analogue warranty. These are called constructor preconditions and they must be satisfied before the constructor is invoked. There are also the post conditions those that will be satisfied by an object off this class after some off its methods has been executed. They are implicit in Java code, but you can imagine that get money back guarantee promises to return unknown null reference. We can promise that because we know that the field will never be now past the constructor. It goes the same with the express warranty fear than its together. Now we see that a Kohler's expectations are fulfilled. The claim warranting method will never fail. That is for sure.

package com;
import java.time.Duration;

```java
import java.time.LocalDate;
import java.time.temporal.ChronoUnit;
public class Demo {
    public void claimWarranty(Article article)
{
        LocalDate today = LocalDate.now();
    if(article.getMoneyBackGuarantee().isValid
On(today)){
     System.out.println("Offer money back");
     }

    if(article.getExpressWarranty().isValidOn(to
day)){
     System.out.println("Offer repair");
     }
        System.out.println("-----------------");
      }
    public void run() {
        Article item1 = new Article();
      }
}
```

And now we come to the entity which constructs the article. Object Constructor is asking for two warranty objects. Let's design some warranties then

```java
package com;
import java.time.Duration;
import java.time.LocalDate;
public class TimeLimitedWarranty
implements Warranty {
    private LocalDate dateIssued;
    private Duration validFor;
```

```java
    public TimeLimitedWarranty(LocalDate
dateIssued, Duration validFor) {
        this.dateIssued = dateIssued;
        this.validFor = validFor;
    }
    @Override
    public boolean isValidOn(LocalDate date)
{
        return this.dateIssued.compareTo(date)
<= 0 &&
this.getExpiredDate.compareTo(date) > 0 ;
    }
    private LocalDate getExpiredDate() {
        return
this.dateIssued.plusDays(this.getValidForDa
ys());
    }
    private long getValidForDays() {
        return this.validFor.toDays();
    }
}
```

This is the model off, a warranted that expires in specified the number of days it receives the issue in date and the duration from which it is valid. The ease, valid on method inherited from the warranty interface is simply comparing the It's to see if the argument falls within the validity interval off this object now back to the place where article constructor was invoked.

```java
package com;
import java.time.Duration;
```

```java
import java.time.LocalDate;
import java.time.temporal.ChronoUnit;
public class Demo {
   public void claimWarranty(Article
article){
               LocalDate today =
LocalDate.now();

if(article.getMoneyBackGuarantee().isValid
On(today)){
  System.out.println("Offer money back");
  }


if(article.getExpressWarranty().isValidOn(to
day)){
  System.out.println("Offer repair");
  }
  System.out.println("-----------------");
}
   public void run() {
      LocalDate sellingDate =
LocalDate.now().minus(40,
ChronoUnit.DAYS);
      Warranty moneyBack1 = new
TimeLimitedWarranty(sellingDate,
Duration.ofDays(60));
      Warranty warranty1 = new
TimeLimitedWarranty(sellingDate,
Duration.ofDays(365));
      Article item1 = new
Article(moneyBack1, warranty1);
```

```
        this.claimWarranty(item1);
    }
}
```

It requests non al warranty reference, so I will obey that precondition. There is nothing else I can do but to pass two objects to the constructor. This code says that the article was sold 40 days ago that it has a money back guarantee within 30 days and an express warranty for free 165 days. The article construction is complete. We're safe from any exceptions. The constructor may throw because we have satisfied. It's preconditions. The claim Warranty methods, preconditions are also satisfied because the article will return no knowledge warranty objects from its public getters. I should be perfectly safe to report a failed article and ask for whatever return I'm illegible to ask for.

```
Main
    "C:\Program Files\AdoptOpenJDK\jdk-8.0.202.08\bin\java.exe" ...
    Offer repair.
    ------------------

Process finished with exit code 0
```

Here you can see that the seller is offering me a repair. That is because a 30 day money back has expired, but regular warranty is still valid. No, not checks around. But that was easier when I had proper warranty objects.

package com;

```java
import java.time.Duration;
import java.time.LocalDate;
import java.time.temporal.ChronoUnit;
public class Demo {
  public void claimWarranty(Article
article){
                LocalDate today =
LocalDate.now();

if(article.getMoneyBackGuarantee().isValid
On(today)){
  System.out.println("Offer money back");
 }


if(article.getExpressWarranty().isValidOn(to
day)){
  System.out.println("Offer repair");
 }
  System.out.println("----------------");
 }
   public void run() {
     LocalDate sellingDate =
LocalDate.now().minus(40,
ChronoUnit.DAYS);
     Warranty moneyBack1 = new
TimeLimitedWarranty(sellingDate,
Duration.ofDays(60));
     Warranty warranty1 = new
TimeLimitedWarranty(sellingDate,
Duration.ofDays(365));
```

```
        Article item1 = new
Article(moneyBack1, warranty1);
     this.claimWarranty(item1);
     Article item2 = new Article(null, null);
// will throw null pointer exception

  }

}
```

Anyway, what if I had an article with no warranty at all? This wouldn't work because the articles constructed will throw the illegal argument exception.

```
Main

"C:\Program Files\AdoptOpenJDK\jdk-8.0.202.08\bin\java.exe" ...
Offer repair.
------------------
Exception in thread "main" java.lang.IllegalArgumentException
    at com.codinghelmet.moreoojava.Article.<init>(Article.java:8)
    at com.codinghelmet.moreoojava.Demo.run(Demo.java:31)
    at com.codinghelmet.moreoojava.Main.main(Main.java:5)

Process finished with exit code 1
```

Precondition violation

We must not violate the classes preconditions when creating its instances.

```
public class Demo {
   public void claimWarranty(Article article)
{
     LocalDate today = LocalDate.now();
     if
(article.getMoneyBackGuarantee().isValidO
n(today)) {
```

```java
        System.out.println("Offer money
back");
    }
    if
(article.getExpressWarranty().isValidOn(tod
ay)) {
        System.out.println("Offer repair");
    }
    System.out.println("-----------------");
  }
  public void run() {
    Article item2 = new Article(null, null); //
provide replacement behavior in methods -->
implement the expected interface --> Replace
nulls with proper objects
    }
}
```

One typical solution to this problem is to devise an object that would stand in place off another reference that substitute object would expose the same public interface and make a full impression that things are happening as expected when its methods are invoked. Look at this idea.

```java
public class VoidWarranty implements
Warranty {
  @Override
  public boolean isValidOn(LocalDate
date){
      return false;
```

```
            }
}
```

Null object pattern
Its objects are doing nothing
But object implements the expected interface

I can define a new class and call it a void
warranty. This is the so called nal object. It
does nothing, but on the flip side it
implements the interface we need and it will
never be now. The only thing void warranty
object will ever do is just say that it is not
valid on whatever date we asked. Now all
objects are normally empty classes. Their
methods have trivial implementations void.
The methods would do nothing. Their body
would be empty, non void methods would
return constants that are telling that there is
nothing special to tell like this false or zero
or an empty string and so on. That is, why
would the normal implemented them as a
single tons.

```
public interface Warranty {
    boolean isValidOn(LocalDate date);

    Warranty VOID = new VoidWarranty();
}
```

In Java, We can expose now objects as
constants on the interface they implement.
Interface variables are static final by
definition. When it comes to consuming a
now object, we can refer to this constant in
any place where a really object is expected.

```java
package com;
import java.time.Duration;
import java.time.LocalDate;
import java.time.temporal.ChronoUnit;
public class Demo {
   public void claimWarranty( Article
article) {
            LocalDate today =
LocalDate.now();

if(article.getMoneyBackGuarantee().isValid
On(today)){
  System.out.println("Offer money back");
  }


if(article.getExpressWarranty().isValidOn(to
day)){
  System.out.println("Offer repair");
  }
  System.out.println("-----------------");
}
   public void run() {
     LocalDate sellingDate =
LocalDate.now().minus(40,
ChronoUnit.DAYS);
     Warranty moneyBack1 = new
TimeLimitedWarranty(sellingDate,
Duration.ofDays(60));
```

```
    Warranty warranty1 = new
TimeLimitedWarranty(sellingDate,
Duration.ofDays(365));
    Article item1 = new
Article(moneyBack1, warranty1);
    this.claimWarranty(item1);
    Article item2 = new
Article(Warranty.VOID, Warranty.VOID);
    this.claimWarranty(item2);
  }
}
```

The last time I was here, the request was that
there are no warranties for the second item.
Fine void warranties will do just fine. It is
really not hard to imagine the world without
now's when you see a demonstration like this
one. Unfortunately, this design only works in
very simple cases, But this use case was
simple anyway,

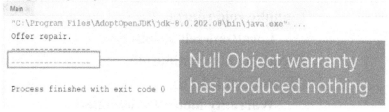

```
Main
"C:\Program Files\AdoptOpenJDK\jdk-8.0.202.08\bin\java.exe" ...
Offer repair.

Process finished with exit code 0
```
Null Object warranty
has produced nothing

And here you can see that new offer was
made when the customer attempted to claim
the warranty. This is a proof of concept that
null references can be replaced with proper
objects. From this point on, we will take a
look at some more complicated execution
scenarios.

Introducing Special Case Objects

```java
public class Demo {
  public void claimWarranty(Article article) {
    LocalDate today = LocalDate.now();
    if (article.getMoneyBackGuarantee().isValidOn(today)) {
      System.out.println("Offer money back");
    }
    if (article.getExpressWarranty().isValidOn(today)) {
      System.out.println("Offer repair");
    }
    System.out.println("-----------------");
  }
  public void run() {
    LocalDate sellingDate = LocalDate.now().minus(40, ChronoUnit.DAYS);
    Warranty moneyBack1 = new TimeLimitedWarranty(sellingDate, Duration.ofDays(60));
    Warranty warranty1 = new TimeLimitedWarranty(sellingDate, Duration.ofDays(365));
```

```
    Article item1 = new
Article(moneyBack1, warranty1); //
alternate behaviours
    this.claimWarranty(item1);
    Article item2 = new
Article(Warranty.VOID,
Warranty.VOID); // alternate behaviours
    this.claimWarranty(item1);
  }
}
```

Null objects have brought polymorphic execution back to the table. Object off. One type indicates one answer to the bully and test. The other object indicates the opposite answer. Therefore, we have no need to test conditions anymore, just excess the object and keep going.

```
public class TimeLimitedWarranty implements Warranty {
```

Concrete implementation
is encapsulated

Possible implementations
Depending on personal information
Depending on article features

```
}
```

Now we can think of more complicated objects. The true beauty of polymorphic design is that the concrete objects can hide

119

the details away. For example, a warranty may be bound to a person, or some specific handling must be applied to the article in order to be eligible to claim warranty. That logic would be implemented in the concrete warranty object.

```java
public class TimeLimitedWarranty
implements Warranty {
   private LocalDate dateIssued;
   private Duration validFor;
   public
TimeLimitedWarranty(LocalDate
dateIssued, Duration validFor) {
      this.dateIssued = dateIssued;
      this.validFor = validFor;
   }
   @Override
   public boolean isValidOn(LocalDate
date){
      return
this.dateIssued.compareTo(date) <= 0 &&

this.getExpiredDate().compareTo(date) >
0;
      }


   private LocalDate getExpiredDate() {
      return
this.dateIssued.plusDays(this.getValidFor
Days());
   }
   private long getValidForDays() {
```

```
        return this.validFor.toDays();
    }
}
```

When it comes to making a claim, we only
need access to this. Peaceful and simple is
valid on method. On the other hand, we
usually have a case or two, which are very
simple in any problem. The main. For
example, what about a lifetime warranty?

```
public class LifetimeWarranty implements Warranty {
    private LocalDate issuedOn;

    public LifetimeWarranty(LocalDate issuedOn) {
        this.issuedOn = issuedOn;
    }

    @Override
    public boolean isValidOn(LocalDate date) {
        return this.issuedOn.compareTo(date) <= 0;
    }
}
```

Special Case pattern

Produces distinct objects
which handle simple special cases
Usually doesn't depend on
domain-related details

It comes with no date at all. Other than
issuing date, it's model would be next to
trivial. Note that this class cannot be
implemented as a nal object because it has a
varying starting big lifetime. Warranty
always has an issuing date, which means that
every instance would be different. That is

121

how we come to the concept of special cases those air the objects that deal with simple, universal special cases. Here is the simplest possible implementation of the lifetime warranty, which doesn't depend on anything from our business domain. There is the principal trade off metal objects in special cases that don't depend on any crosses and logic that belonged to the domain model. The only depend on core abstractions like this warranty interface. And then we can conveniently expose all of them for the abstraction itself.

```
public interface Warranty {
    boolean isValidOn(LocalDate date);

    Warranty VOID = new VoidWarranty();

    static Warranty lifetime(LocalDate issuedOn) {
        return new LifetimeWarranty(issuedOn);
    }
}
```

The interface itself and a few now objects and special case implementations can be packaged together. There, the rest of the domain model, the gruesome, complex tangle, the classes and interfaces can be packaged separately. They were consumed these lightweight objects as utilities as helpers and substitutes for more complex objects where appropriate.

```
public class Demo {
    public void claimWarranty(Article article) {
        LocalDate today = LocalDate.now();

        if (article.getMoneyBackGuarantee().isValidOn(today)) {
            System.out.println("Offer money back.");
        }

        if (article.getExpressWarranty().isValidOn(today)) {
            System.out.println("Offer repair.");
        }

        System.out.println("-----------------");
    }

    public void run() {
        LocalDate sellingDate = LocalDate.now().minus( amountToSubtract 40, ChronoUnit.DAYS);
        Warranty moneyBack1 = new TimeLimitedWarranty(sellingDate, Duration.ofDays(30));
        Warranty warranty1 = new TimeLimitedWarranty(sellingDate, Duration.ofDays(365));

        Article item1 = new Article(moneyBack1, warranty1);

        this.claimWarranty(item1);

        Article item2 = new Article(Warranty.VOID, Warranty.lifetime(sellingDate));
        this.claimWarranty(item2);
    }
}
```

In this demo, I can issue a lifetime warranty without having to know any technical details about the sale or about the buyer. I will mention an example where this idea with special case objects is very useful.

Special Case Pattern Example

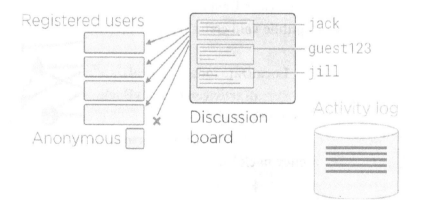

On e commerce website, we can keep record of registered users and use the accumulated data been implementing different activities on the website. But we can also use a lightweight object representing an anonymous user instead, maybe only carrying a temporary nickname and nothing else. When it comes to recording activity, this special case object will simply produce nothing Toby recorded. On the other hand, anonymous user object could post messages on the discussion board only without the ability to subscribe to notifications because we obviously don't know how to contact such a user.

Turning Boolean Methods into Filters

By this point, we have turned the entire logic related to warranties into book. Tow.

```
public class Demo {
    public void claimWarranty(Article article)
{
    LocalDate today = LocalDate.now();
        if(article.getMoneyBackGuarantee(
).isValidOn(today)){
            System.out.println("Offer
money back.");
        }
```

```java
        if(article.getExpressWarranty().isV
alidOn(today)){
                System.out.println("Offer
repair.");
        }
    System.out.println("----------------");
  }
  public void run() {
    LocalDate sellingDate =
LocalDate.now().minus(40,
ChronoUnit.DAYS);
        Warranty moneyBack1 = new
TimeLimitedWarranty(sellingDate,
Duration.ofDays(60));
        Warranty warranty1 = new
TimeLimitedWarranty(sellingDate,
Duration.ofDays(365));
        Article item1 = new
Article(moneyBack1, warranty1);
        this.claimWarranty(item1);
        Article item2 = new
Article(Warranty.VOID,
Warranty.lifetime(sellingDate));
        this.claimWarranty(item2);
  }
}
```

This single is valid on method, but a problem
is that we're still branching over its result.
What is the purpose of turning everything
into object if we only use those objects to
feed the if instruction? The key to solving
our problems is in understanding that

warranty objects are not really doing anything. They're just helping me to branch, leaving me to implement operations all by myself.

```
public interface Warranty {
    boolean isValidOn(LocalDate date);

    Warranty VOID = new VoidWarranty();

    static Warranty lifetime(LocalDate issuedOn) {
        return new LifetimeWarranty(issuedOn);
    }
}
```

- Boolean method is a design flaw.
- Do not tell the caller when to do something .
- Expose the proper operation instead.

Beware off this trap that is the most common mistake. An object oriented programming. We use objects only as guides or helpers while implementing complete operations on the calling end. That is wrong. Operations should entirely be in object today concern. How do we claim a warranted than we claim it?

```
public interface Warranty {
    boolean isValidOn(LocalDate date);
    void claim();

    Warranty VOID = new VoidWarranty();

    static Warranty lifetime(LocalDate issuedOn) {
        return new LifetimeWarranty(issuedOn);
    }
}
```

By taking the warranty object and telling it, Go claim yourself. That is the object oriented way again. The consumer it used to branch over the Boolean method result.

```java
public class Demo {
    public void claimWarranty(Article article) {
        LocalDate today = LocalDate.now();

        article.getMoneyBackGuarantee().claim();



        if(article.getExpressWarranty().isValidOn(today)){
            System.out.println("Offer repair.");
        }
        System.out.println("----------------");
    }
    public void run() {
        LocalDate sellingDate = LocalDate.now().minus(40, ChronoUnit.DAYS);
        Warranty moneyBack1 = new TimeLimitedWarranty(sellingDate, Duration.ofDays(60));
        Warranty warranty1 = new TimeLimitedWarranty(sellingDate, Duration.ofDays(365));
        Article item1 = new Article(moneyBack1, warranty1);
        this.claimWarranty(item1);
```

```
    Article item2 = new
Article(Warranty.VOID,
Warranty.lifetime(sellingDate));
    this.claimWarranty(item2);
  }
}
```

Now I want to stop thinking about two
distinct behaviors like claimed the warranty
or don't. The only responsibility of this
method is to effectively claim a warranty.
Looks like magic, right, and it is a bit of
magic because this piece of code cannot be
realistically expected to work. First off, all
the report date has been lost. Second, the
action which should be taken when
warranties valid is also lost. Back to the
drawing table.

```
public interface Warranty {
    boolean isValidOn(LocalDate date);
    default void claim(Runnable action) { action.run(); }

    Warranty VOID = new VoidWarranty();

    static Warranty lifetime(LocalDate issuedOn) {
        return new LifetimeWarranty(issuedOn);
    }
}
```

Claim method will receive a call back to
execute. I will use the Runa Ble interface for
this purpose. It exposes the run method
which receives no arguments and returns
void. I can't even provided the default
implementation here so that concrete classes
do not have to worry about it. A call back.

```java
public class VoidWarranty implements Warranty {
    @Override
    public boolean isValidOn(LocalDate date) {
        return false;
    }

    @Override
    public void claim(Runnable action) { }
}
```

The only warranty which does not executed the claim callback is the void warranty. It will implement an anti claim method, and by that simple trick, we will effectively implemented the else branch, the branch which executes when warranty is not applicable.

```java
public interface Warranty {
    boolean isValidOn(LocalDate date);
    Warranty on(LocalDate date);
    default void claim(Runnable action) { action.run(); }

    Warranty VOID = new VoidWarranty();

    static Warranty lifetime(LocalDate issuedOn) {
        return new LifetimeWarranty(issuedOn);
    }
}
```

The Filtering API Style

Removes the need for Boolean methods

Returns the *version* of an object given a condition

Makes subsequent calls *unconditional*

Concrete classes should focus on a more substantial behavior filtering warranties by day. This is the functional style which are usually called the filtering API. I will not be asking the warranty object to tell whether it is applicability. Given date or not, I'm turning the table and now I'm asking the warranty object to give me the version off itself on a given date. Then I plan to call the claim a method unconditionally on the result Off this filter, let me show you what it will look like on the time limited warranty.

```java
public class TimeLimitedWarranty
implements Warranty {
   private LocalDate dateIssued;
   private Duration validFor;
   public TimeLimitedWarranty(LocalDate
dateIssued, Duration validFor) {
      this.dateIssued = dateIssued;
      this.validFor = validFor;
   }
      private boolean iaValidOn(LocalDate
date) {
      return this.dateIssued.compareTo(date)
<= 0 &&

this.getExpiredDate().compareTo(date) > 0;
   }

   @Override
   public Warranty on(LocalDate date) {
      return date.compareTo(this.dateIssued)
< 0 ? Warranty.VOID
         :
date.compareTo(this.getExpiredDate()) > 0 ?
Warranty.VOID
         : this;
   }
}
```
What it does the time limited warranty looks
like on any date. I'll tell you what it looks
like before it was issued. It looks the same is
the void warranty. After it expires, it will
look the same. Otherwise, it is a perfectly

valid warranty and it will look the way it normally looks. You may complain that I have replaced one branching with another branching and you would be right to an extent. This branching is performed around the argument which cannot be predicted. That is the valid reason to branches. This branching instruction cannot be replaced with any unconditional operation. On the other hand, this branching is performed inside the future producer. No consumer will ever see it.

```java
public class Demo {
   private void offerMoneyBack() {
     System.out.println("Offer money back.");
   }
   private void offerRepair() {
     System.out.println("Offer repair.");
   }
   public void claimWarranty(Article article) {
       LocalDate today = LocalDate.now();

article.getMoneyBackGuarantee().on(today).claim(this::offerMoneyBack);

article.getExpressWarranty().on(today).claim(this::offerRepair);
     System.out.println("----------------");
   }
   public void run() {
```

```java
        LocalDate sellingDate =
LocalDate.now().minus(40,
ChronoUnit.DAYS);
        Warranty moneyBack1 = new
TimeLimitedWarranty(sellingDate,
Duration.ofDays(60));
        Warranty warranty1 = new
TimeLimitedWarranty(sellingDate,
Duration.ofDays(365));
        Article item1 = new
Article(moneyBack1, warranty1);
        this.claimWarranty(item1);
        Article item2 = new
Article(Warranty.VOID,
Warranty.lifetime(sellingDate));
        this.claimWarranty(item2);
    }
}
```

Future consumer will perform its part unconditionally. No branching under consuming end and the claim will be made unconditionally. Thanks to the callback, Baron over repeated the same process with the second warrant. Did I promise a non branching implementation of the claim warranty method here it is unknown. Branching implementation Shin I never needed branching under consuming, and that is the truth.

```java
public class LifetimeWarranty implements
Warranty {
    private LocalDate issuedOn;
```

```
public LifetimeWarranty(LocalDate
issuedOn) {
    this.issuedOn = issuedOn;
}

private boolean iaValidOn(LocalDate
date) {
    return this.issuedOn.compareTo(date)
<= 0 ;
}

@Override
public Warranty on(LocalDate date) {
    return date.compareTo(this.issuedOn) <
0 ? Warranty.VOID : this;
}
}
```

Let's complete concrete warrant is then lifetime warranty will be void before it's issuing date. Otherwise, it will pass the filtering and return itself.

```
public class VoidWarranty implements Warranty {
    @Override
    public boolean isValidOn(LocalDate date) {
        return false;
    }

    @Override
    public void claim(Runnable action) { }

    @Override
    public Warranty on(LocalDate date) { return this; }
}
```

Finally, void. Warranty will always be void. This completes implementation of all concrete warranties, claiming the warrant is

**that implemented without need for
branching with design. Based on filtering
methods like this on method, we have no
need for methods returning boolean**

```
public interface Warranty {
    Warranty on(LocalDate date);
    default void claim(Runnable action) { action.run(); }

    Warranty VOID = new VoidWarranty();

    static Warranty lifetime(LocalDate issuedOn) {
        return new LifetimeWarranty(issuedOn);
    }
}
```

**To improve the design, I will remove the
boolean method entirely.
public class LifetimeWarranty implements
Warranty {
    private LocalDate issuedOn;
    public LifetimeWarranty(LocalDate
issuedOn) {
        this.issuedOn = issuedOn;
    }
    @Override
    public Warranty on(LocalDate date) {
        return date.compareTo(this.issuedOn) <
0 ? Warranty.VOID : this;
    }
}
public class TimeLimitedWarranty
implements Warranty {
    private LocalDate dateIssued;
    private Duration validFor;
    public TimeLimitedWarranty(LocalDate
dateIssued, Duration validFor) {**

```java
    this.dateIssued = dateIssued;
    this.validFor = validFor;
  }
  @Override
  public Warranty on(LocalDate date) {
    return date.compareTo(this.dateIssued)
< 0 ? Warranty.VOID
        :
date.compareTo(this.getExpiredDate()) > 0 ?
Warranty.VOID
        : this;
  }
  private LocalDate getExpiredDate() {
    return
this.dateIssued.plusDays(this.getValidForDa
ys());
  }
  private long getValidForDays() {
    return this.validFor.toDays();
  }
}
public class VoidWarranty implements
Warranty {
  @Override
  public void claim(Runnable action) { }
  @Override
  public Warranty on(LocalDate date) {
return this; }
}
```

Concrete warranty classes do not need it, either. There's no trace of boolean type remaining in the whole solution.

```
Main
"C:\Program Files\AdoptOpenJDK\jdk
Offer repair.
-------------------
Offer repair.
-------------------

Process finished with exit code 0
```

The application will offer repair to the
customer as expected. That's still, we have
lost the feature that used to exist before in
this demo. I'm not reporting the state of the
article. Let's insert that feature back into the
design

Turning an Object into a Finite State Machine

public class Article {

   private Warranty moneyBackGuarantee;

   private Warranty expressWarranty;

   private Article(Warranty
moneyBackGuarantee, Warranty
expressWarranty) {

     if (moneyBackGuarantee == null) throw
new IllegalArgumentException();

     if (expressWarranty == null) throw new
IllegalArgumentException();

     this.moneyBackGuarantee =
moneyBackGuarantee;

137

```
    this.expressWarranty =
expressWarranty;
    }
    public Warranty
getMoneyBackGuarantee() { return
moneyBackGuarantee; }
    public Warranty getExpressWarranty() {
return effectiveExpressWarranty; }
}
```
Customer requests :

- **Moneyback - not visible damage**
- **Repair - not operational**

At the beginning of this module we used
apply additional criteria to decide whether a
warrant is Africa below or not. Money back
guarantee holds If there are no visible wear
and tear marks, repair is offered for articles
that are not operational. I said that these
rules will be part of the article itself because
in object oriented programming, objects
should keep track off their state. But the way
I wish to implement this feature might
surprise you. I will turn the article into finite
state machine.

```java
package com;
public class Article {
    private Warranty moneyBackGuarantee;
    private Warranty expressWarranty;
    private Warranty
effectiveExpressWarranty;
    public Article(Warranty
moneyBackGuarantee, Warranty
expressWarranty) {
        this(moneyBackGuarantee,
expressWarranty, Warranty.VOID);
    }
    private Article(Warranty
moneyBackGuarantee, Warranty
expressWarranty, Warranty
effectiveExpressWarranty) {
        if (moneyBackGuarantee == null) throw
new IllegalArgumentException();
        if (expressWarranty == null) throw new
IllegalArgumentException();
        this.moneyBackGuarantee =
moneyBackGuarantee;
        this.expressWarranty =
expressWarranty;
        this.effectiveExpressWarranty =
effectiveExpressWarranty;
    }
    public Warranty
getMoneyBackGuarantee() { return
moneyBackGuarantee; }
```

```
    public Warranty getExpressWarranty() {
return effectiveExpressWarranty; }
    public Article withVisibleDamage() {
        return new Article(Warranty.VOID,
this.expressWarranty,
this.effectiveExpressWarranty);
    }
    public Article notOperational() {
        return new
Article(this.moneyBackGuarantee,
this.expressWarranty,
this.expressWarranty);
    }
}
```

What is this money back guarantee? Is it
really the guarantee that we will offer? Yes.
Unless there is damage on the item, the
article could expose a method to report a
visible damage. In previous module. We have
talked at full length about the benefits of
mutability. This demo is the opportunity to
practice what we have learned. Back then.
This method will return a fresh, immutable
copy of the article which will carry
remembrance of visible damage inflicted to
it. Hence, the new instance will differ. But in
what respect? I'm glad that this question has

popped up because I know the answer. It will be the same is current instance, except that its money back guarantee will be void no matter what guarantee it waas in the new state, there will be no money back. Do tow a visible damage. I like this principle a lot. It is usually simple to implement, and it produces objects which are especially easy to manage. Let's practice some more this time with express warranty the same design as in the case of money back guarantee. Only this time the situation is opposite. When the device stops working, the guarantee should become non void. Funny enough regularly. Warranty doesn't apply before something bad happens to the article, so that may look like a complicated requirement. But in fact it is very simple. If we stick to the idea that the article is a state machine. In that sense, express warrant itself is not effective. Effective warranties void when the article begins its life because there's nothing wrong with it. Now we need to manage the effective warranty that we create a private constructor for death. I have used the opportunity to remove coat duplication. Private constructor is the most detailed one, and public constructor will delegate to it, changing the state when article is not operational means to make express warranty effective. It also means that money back guarantee remains in place. By the way, I will help to fix the first method. Now any effective warranty must be preserved because visible damage does not affect it. That is all power requirements, and now it's lost the pinnacle of this whole redesign. The express warrant together will not return the express warranty. That may sound like a joke, but I assure you that I'm serious about this. You might protest, saying that express warrant together is the gether for the express warranty field. At least that's what the books are teaching. There's a field and there is a gather for that field. But then I might ask you, just out of curiosity, how enough do you know that there is a private field named Express Warrant in this class? Seriously express warranties and encapsulated concept. I am exposing a public together for death kind off warranty, but I'm not exposing the formula, which is calculating it. I may change my mind in the future or forgets the future. I have changed it a minute ago. That is how encapsulation works. An object oriented programming. I promise to maintain the public together in the future. But I do not promise that Internal state will remain the same. That is why I'm keeping it private.

```
public class Demo {
  private void offerMoneyBack() {
    System.out.println("Offer money back.");
  }
  private void offerRepair() {
    System.out.println("Offer repair.");
  }
  public void claimWarranty(Article article) {
    LocalDate today = LocalDate.now();

article.getMoneyBackGuarantee().on(today).claim(this::offerMoneyBack);

article.getExpressWarranty().on(today).claim(this::offerRepair);
    System.out.println("----------------");
  }
  public void run() {
    LocalDate sellingDate = LocalDate.now().minus(40, ChronoUnit.DAYS);
```

```java
        Warranty moneyBack1 = new
TimeLimitedWarranty(sellingDate,
Duration.ofDays(60));
        Warranty warranty1 = new
TimeLimitedWarranty(sellingDate,
Duration.ofDays(365));
        Article item1 = new
Article(moneyBack1, warranty1);
        this.claimWarranty(item1);
        Article item2 = new
Article(Warranty.VOID,
Warranty.lifetime(sellingDate));
        this.claimWarranty(item2);
    }
}
```

When I implemented the new requirement,
this caller has remained the same even more.
The new requirement will be observed right
here in this line of code which I haven't
changed. The meaning off encapsulation is to
expose behavior, not data. That way your
code will be easier to maintain. As you have
seen in this example, let me run the
application.

Main

"C:\Program Files\AdoptOpenJDK\jdk-8.0.202.08\bin\java.exe" ...

Process finished with exit code 0

Now look, there's nothing on the outward. All warranties are off. Money back guarantee is off because it has expired and repair was not offered because the article was not broken in the first place. I will now shake this demo a bit so that you can get sense off all the features we have in this final design.

```java
package com;
import java.time.Duration;
import java.time.LocalDate;
import java.time.temporal.ChronoUnit;
public class Demo {
    private void offerMoneyBack() {
        System.out.println("Offer money back.");
    }
    private void offerRepair() {
        System.out.println("Offer repair.");
    }
    public void claimWarranty(Article article)
    {
        LocalDate today = LocalDate.now();

article.getMoneyBackGuarantee().on(today).claim(this::offerMoneyBack);

article.getExpressWarranty().on(today).claim(this::offerRepair);
        System.out.println("----------------");
```

```java
    }
    public void run() {
        LocalDate sellingDate =
LocalDate.now().minus(40,
ChronoUnit.DAYS);
        Warranty moneyBack1 = new
TimeLimitedWarranty(sellingDate,
Duration.ofDays(60));
        Warranty warranty1 = new
TimeLimitedWarranty(sellingDate,
Duration.ofDays(365));
        Article item1 = new
Article(moneyBack1, warranty1);
        this.claimWarranty(item1);

    this.claimWarranty(item1.withVisibleDama
ge());

this.claimWarranty(item1.notOperational().
withVisibleDamage());

this.claimWarranty(item1.notOperational());
        Article item2 = new
Article(Warranty.VOID,
Warranty.lifetime(sellingDate));
     this.claimWarranty(item2);

this.claimWarranty(item2.withVisibleDamag
e().notOperational());
    }
}
```

Let's extend money back for 60 days and then I will claim warranties for all states of the product imaginable.

```
Main
"C:\Program Files\AdoptOpenJDK\jd)
Offer money back.
------------------------

------------------------
Offer repair.
------------------
Offer money back.
Offer repair.

------------------

------------------
Offer repair.
------------------

Process finished with exit code 0
```

Let's walk for the output and compare it to code money Back will be offered for a perfectly good product. That is correct. Money back will not be offered for a product with visible damage that is correct. Repair will be offered for non operational product but no money back because it is also damaged. Good for a non operational product, which is also in good condition. Both money, back and repair are the options. Finally, I have switched order, of course, on the second product, just to show you that death. It doesn't make any difference. Repair was offered, but no money back because if for no other reason, this product doesn't even come with money back offer. I hope that you will find this demonstration useful. Not only that, I have removed all null references, but I have also managed to remove all branching instructions in the consuming Cole. There are more edge cases where it might have looked like we must fall back to using all references. We will cover those cases in the next module, and with that, we will put to the whole question off. Now's to an end. There will be no null references, and that is it. Before that, let's briefly summarize what we have learned so far.

Summary

Techniques to remove null references
- Remove branching around null
- Null Object instances with empty implementation
- Special Case instances with trivial implementation
- All together help eradicate nulls

In this module, we have seen a group of related techniques that can be used to avoid the using in our references. And when I say using now lt's I mean branching around the null conditions because there is no way to really use null reference. You can only guard against accidentally the referencing it you have seen and now object substitute objects that can provide empty implementation off methods we need. In other cases, the substitute implementation might not be entirely empty, but the object would still be simple. We call such objects special cases as they're handing well, special cases for us with the null objects, special case objects and full blown objects. It is possible to implement entire pieces of functionality without ever having another reference appear anywhere in code and with no branching around null, too.

Object as a finite state machine (FSM)
- Expose unconditional methods
- Encapsulated state drives behavior
- It requires no branching in the caller

By the end of the module, you have learned a related technique for evading branching. An object can be turned into an encapsulated finished state machine and then expose unconditional methods that exhibit abstract to the main behavior. Slight variations in behavior are controlled by the current

149

private state of the object, but without explicit branching.

Relating FSM to the State pattern
- Each concrete state is a separate class
- FSM manages state as a set of objects
- FSM looks polymorphic to the outside

If you remember the demo with bank account states early in this book, each state there was modelled as a separate class implementing the same interface. The state machine technique from this module is very similar. Only the state variation is implemented inside a single class. We could call this technique a lightweight polymorphism. This completes the first half of the analysis off null references. In the next module, we will keep going in the same direction by covering optional objects, objects that might exist or might not exist. With that powerful design technique, you will never fear the urge to assign null to a reference.

Module 6 : Turning Optional Calls into Calls on Optional Objects

Understanding the Need to Model Missing Objects

Now object and special case our nice little tricks that can help reduce the need to pass null references around. But sooner or later you will face a problem in which there is no substitute object that will do the trick. In this module we will talk about optional objects, objects that may or may not be, if you have been using null references as the only way to indicate missing objects than this module is the right place for you.

```
package com;
public class Article {
    private Warranty moneyBackGuarantee;
    private Warranty expressWarranty;
    private Warranty
effectiveExpressWarranty;
    public Article(Warranty
moneyBackGuarantee, Warranty
expressWarranty) {
        this(moneyBackGuarantee,
expressWarranty, Warranty.VOID);
```

```
    }
    private Article(Warranty
moneyBackGuarantee, Warranty
expressWarranty, Warranty
effectiveExpressWarranty) {
        this.moneyBackGuarantee =
moneyBackGuarantee;
        this.expressWarranty =
expressWarranty;
        this.effectiveExpressWarranty =
effectiveExpressWarranty;
    }
    public Warranty
getMoneyBackGuarantee() { return
moneyBackGuarantee; }
    public Warranty getExpressWarranty() {
return effectiveExpressWarranty; }
    public Article withVisibleDamage() {
        return new Article(Warranty.VOID,
this.expressWarranty,
this.effectiveExpressWarranty);
    }
    public Article notOperational() {
        return new
Article(this.moneyBackGuarantee,
this.expressWarranty,
this.expressWarranty);
    }
}
```

Here we are again. In the same example
from the previous module. An article is
associated with warranties. Now imagine

that some articles are coming with replaceable electrical parts, which are also subject to a warranty.

```java
package com;
import java.time.LocalDate;
public class Part {
    private LocalDate installmentDate; // Date when the part was installed
    private LocalDate defectDetectedOn; // Date when the defect was diagnosed and here, null == OK
    public Part(LocalDate installmentDate) {
        this(installmentDate, null);
    }
    private Part(LocalDate installmentDate, LocalDate defectDetectedOn) {
        this.installmentDate = installmentDate;
        this.defectDetectedOn = defectDetectedOn;
    }
    public Part defective(LocalDate detectedOn) {
        return new Part(this.installmentDate, detectedOn);
    }
}
```

This is the class named Part. It is modeling. A replaceable part installed on some date. Part which may have failed on another date, noted that another failure date models apart, which is operational when a defect is discovered. The date is set to a non null value.

```java
package com;
import java.time.LocalDate;
public class Article {
    private Warranty moneyBackGuarantee;
    private Warranty expressWarranty;
    private Warranty
effectiveExpressWarranty;
    private Part sensor;
    private Warranty extendedWarranty;
    public Article(Warranty
moneyBackGuarantee, Warranty
expressWarranty) {
        this(moneyBackGuarantee,
expressWarranty, Warranty.VOID, null,
Warranty.VOID);
    }
    private Article(
        Warranty moneyBackGuarantee,
        Warranty expressWarranty,
        Warranty effectiveExpressWarranty,
        Part sensor, Warranty
extendedWarranty) {
        this.moneyBackGuarantee =
moneyBackGuarantee;
        this.expressWarranty =
expressWarranty;
        this.effectiveExpressWarranty =
effectiveExpressWarranty;
        this.sensor = sensor;
```

```java
        this.extendedWarranty =
extendedWarranty;
    }
    public Warranty
getMoneyBackGuarantee() { return
this.moneyBackGuarantee; }
    public Warranty getExpressWarranty() {
return this.effectiveExpressWarranty; }
    public Article withVisibleDamage() {
        return new Article(Warranty.VOID,
this.expressWarranty,
this.effectiveExpressWarranty,
                this.sensor,
this.extendedWarranty);
    }
    public Article notOperational() {
        return new
Article(this.moneyBackGuarantee,
this.expressWarranty, this.expressWarranty,
                this.sensor,
this.extendedWarranty);
    }
    public Article install(Part sensor,
Warranty extendedWarranty) {
        return new
Article(this.moneyBackGuarantee,
this.expressWarranty,
this.effectiveExpressWarranty,
                sensor, extendedWarranty);
    }
}
```

Customer request

Sensor warranty is effective on detection date, not on repair date

As per requirement. Some articles were selling. Will hella sends are installed. The trick is that this part comes with a warranty off its own, noted that now sensor indicates that apart was not installed to install it. I will open even more arguments in the private constructor. This implementation is symptomatic the argument. The list has grown beyond reasonable limits long ago. While now is used to steer behavior, I have very started and everything is already wrong. But still, I will try to live with this design a little longer. Arguments, arguments. And then comes the method, which installs new sensor. The interesting part is that the circuitry may fail and the warranty will be claimed with the date when failure was detected rather than the date when the device was brought in for repair.

```java
package com;
import java.time.LocalDate;
public class Article {
    private Warranty moneyBackGuarantee;
    private Warranty expressWarranty;
    private Warranty
effectiveExpressWarranty;
    private Part sensor;
    private Warranty extendedWarranty;
```

```java
    public Article(Warranty
moneyBackGuarantee, Warranty
expressWarranty) {
    this(moneyBackGuarantee,
expressWarranty, Warranty.VOID, null,
Warranty.VOID);
    }
    private Article(
    Warranty moneyBackGuarantee,
    Warranty expressWarranty,
    Warranty effectiveExpressWarranty,
    Part sensor, Warranty
extendedWarranty) {
    this.moneyBackGuarantee =
moneyBackGuarantee;
    this.expressWarranty =
expressWarranty;
    this.effectiveExpressWarranty =
effectiveExpressWarranty;
    this.sensor = sensor;
    this.extendedWarranty =
extendedWarranty;
    }
    public Warranty
getMoneyBackGuarantee() { return
this.moneyBackGuarantee; }
    public Warranty getExpressWarranty() {
return this.effectiveExpressWarranty; }
    public Warranty getExtendedWarranty()
{
    if(sensor == null) return Warranty.VOID ;
```

```java
    LocalDate detectedOn =
this.sensor.getDefectDetectedOn();
    if(detectedOn == null) return
Warranty.VOID ;
        return
this.extendedWarranty)).on(detectedOn);
    }
    public Article withVisibleDamage() {
        return new Article(Warranty.VOID,
this.expressWarranty,
this.effectiveExpressWarranty,
                    this.sensor,
this.extendedWarranty);
    }
    public Article notOperational() {
        return new
Article(this.moneyBackGuarantee,
this.expressWarranty, this.expressWarranty,
                    this.sensor,
this.extendedWarranty);
    }
    public Article install(Part sensor,
Warranty extendedWarranty) {
        return new
Article(this.moneyBackGuarantee,
this.expressWarranty,
this.effectiveExpressWarranty,
                    sensor, extendedWarranty);
    }
    public Article
sensorNotOperational(LocalDate
detectedOn) {
```

```
        return
this.install(this.sensor.defective(detectedOn),
this.extendedWarranty));
    }
}
```

Let's see what complications will come out of that new rule. The sensor, not operational method will be called when an issue is detected. A new sensor object will model the failed part, and the parts current warranty will be retained. Another method will be there to claim warranty. That will be the cherry on top of this gruesome design, claiming the extended warranty happens on the date when the failure was detected. This date could be now if there is no failure date than there is no warranty I'm branching around the now again. By the way, I almost forgot that there might not be the sensor in the first place that was close. There was a back there. Did you see? That is what happens and flow is controlled with now's. Now I have free branches around the null references and exposure of private data that is unacceptable. You should train your eye to dismiss code like this and start it all over again right away.

```
package com;
import java.time.LocalDate;
public class Article {
    private Warranty moneyBackGuarantee;
    private Warranty expressWarranty;
```

```java
    private Warranty
effectiveExpressWarranty;
    private Part sensor;
    private Warranty extendedWarranty;
    public Article(Warranty
moneyBackGuarantee, Warranty
expressWarranty) {
        this(moneyBackGuarantee,
expressWarranty, Warranty.VOID, null,
Warranty.VOID);
    }
    private Article(
        Warranty moneyBackGuarantee,
        Warranty expressWarranty,
        Warranty effectiveExpressWarranty,
        Part sensor, Warranty
extendedWarranty) {
        this.moneyBackGuarantee =
moneyBackGuarantee;
        this.expressWarranty =
expressWarranty;
        this.effectiveExpressWarranty =
effectiveExpressWarranty;
        this.sensor = sensor;
        this.extendedWarranty =
extendedWarranty;
    }
    public Warranty
getMoneyBackGuarantee() { return
this.moneyBackGuarantee; }
    public Warranty getExpressWarranty() {
return this.effectiveExpressWarranty; }
```

```java
    public Warranty getExtendedWarranty()
{
 return this.sensor == null ? Warranty.VOID
 : this.sensor.apply(this.extendedWarranty);
    }
    public Article withVisibleDamage() {
        return new Article(Warranty.VOID,
this.expressWarranty,
this.effectiveExpressWarranty,
                    this.sensor,
this.extendedWarranty);
    }
    public Article notOperational() {
        return new
Article(this.moneyBackGuarantee,
this.expressWarranty, this.expressWarranty,
                    this.sensor,
this.extendedWarranty);
    }
    public Article install(Part sensor,
Warranty extendedWarranty) {
        return new
Article(this.moneyBackGuarantee,
this.expressWarranty,
this.effectiveExpressWarranty,
                sensor, extendedWarranty);
    }
    public Article
sensorNotOperational(LocalDate
detectedOn) {
```

```
      return
this.install(this.sensor.defective(detectedOn),
this.extendedWarranty));
   }
}
```

What I really want is to return no warranty if there is no sensor war. Otherwise left the sensor object to decide on warranty based on its encapsulated state. There's still branching around now, and I will get back to it in due time. The rest of the complexity has been removed

```
public class Part {
   private LocalDate installmentDate;
   private LocalDate defectDetectedOn;
   public Part(LocalDate installmentDate)
{
     this(installmentDate, null);
   }
   private Part(LocalDate installmentDate,
LocalDate defectDetectedOn) {
     this.installmentDate =
installmentDate;
     this.defectDetectedOn =
defectDetectedOn;
   }
     public LocalDate
getDefectDetectedOn(){
         return this.defectDetectedOn;
   }
```

```java
    public Part defective(LocalDate
detectedOn) {
        return new Part(this.installmentDate,
detectedOn);
    }
    public Warranty apply(Warranty
partWarranty) {
        return this.defectDetectedOn == null
? Warranty.VOID
        :
Warranty.lifetime(this.defectDetectedOn);
    }
}
```

Inside the part class. The logic will be very similar. Onley observed that this piece of code is doing more. If there is no defected attraction date, then there is no warranty. Otherwise, I knew warranty model is issued, the one which begins on the detection date and lasts forever. The article can be brought to a repair desk at any later date, and it will still be eligible for a free sensor replacement. Those are the little gift you get back from a consistent design.

```java
public class Demo {
    private void offerMoneyBack() {
        System.out.println("Offer money
back.");
    }
    private void offerRepair() {
        System.out.println("Offer repair.");
    }
```

```java
    private void offerSensorRepair() {
System.out.println("Offer sensor
replacement."); }
    private void claimWarranty(Article
article) {
        LocalDate today = LocalDate.now();

article.getMoneyBackGuarantee().on(toda
y).claim(this::offerMoneyBack);

article.getExpressWarranty().on(today).cl
aim(this::offerRepair);

article.getExtendedWarranty().on(today).c
laim(this::offerSensorRepair);
        System.out.println("--------------------
");
    }
    public void run() {
        LocalDate sellingDate =
LocalDate.now().minus(40,
ChronoUnit.DAYS);
        Warranty moneyBack = new
TimeLimitedWarranty(sellingDate,
Duration.ofDays(60));
        Warranty warranty = new
TimeLimitedWarranty(sellingDate,
Duration.ofDays(365));
        Part sensor = new Part(sellingDate);
        Warranty sensorWarranty = new
TimeLimitedWarranty(sellingDate,
Duration.ofDays(90));
```

```
        Article item = new
Article(moneyBack,
warranty).install(sensor,
sensorWarranty);
        this.claimWarranty(item);

this.claimWarranty(item.withVisibleDama
ge());

this.claimWarranty(item.notOperational().
withVisibleDamage());

this.claimWarranty(item.notOperational()
);
        LocalDate sensorExamined =
LocalDate.now().minus(2,
ChronoUnit.DAYS);

this.claimWarranty(item.sensorNotOperat
ional(sensorExamined));

this.claimWarranty(item.notOperational().
sensorNotOperational(sensorExamined));
    }
}
```

Let's try to use this model, Ben. This is the
same demonstration as we had it in the
previous module. I will install a sensor
claiming the sensor warranty will be no
different than any other. That is the charm
of this design. It is still perfectly consistent.
All claims are following the same protocol.

Finally, we can simulate sensor failure detected two days ago. Let's see how our classes will cope with this request.

```
Main
"C:\Program Files\AdoptOpenJDK\jdk-8.0.202.08\bin\java.exe" ...
Offer money back.
--------------------
--------------------

Offer repair.
--------------------
Offer money back.
Offer repair.
--------------------
Offer money back.
Offer sensor replacement.
--------------------
Offer money back.
Offer repair.
Offer sensor replacement.
--------------------

Process finished with exit code 0
```

In the first example sends a replacement is offered along with refund. In the second example, the whole device is out of order on top of having a broken sensor. Therefore, repair sends a replacement, and money back are all in the game. This was the first attempt to control code complexity when some objects might not exist. From this point on, we will examine the issues in this solution and then fix them with an improved, object oriented design

Looking for a Bug? Then Look for a Null

Polymorphic Call vs. Branching :

```
var service = producerA;        void f(value) {
service.do();                       if (value > 5)
                                        executeA();
...                                 else
                                        executeB();
var service = producerB;
var selector = useA;

if (selector == useA)
  this.executeA();
else
  this.executeB();
...
var selector = useB;
```

In object oriented programming, we can sometimes implement conditional logic by substituting objects. If we are invoking a virtual method on an object than actual invocation, target is unknown. It compiled

167

time only at RunTime dynamic dispatch mechanism will effectively perform the branching for us and decide which actual matter to invoke. If we didn't have this mechanism at our disposal, we would have to code entire if else instruction and do the branching ourselves. The reference to an object is the living result of the boolean expression over which we would otherwise branch when conditions change such that this imaginary boolean expressions result. With the change, we immediately substituted the object with the one which represents the new outcome. That is how the reference to an object is playing the role of the result off a Boolean expression. Whenever we touch an object, we can rest assured that that object is just right for our current situation. That is how we can effectively eliminate most of the branching instructions that only depend on the interstate of the object. Unfortunately, we cannot remove branching instructions that depend on input arguments off a method we can only react on argument values once we receive them. And that is why some of the branching instructions will remain.

```java
public Warranty getExtendedWarranty() {
    return this.sensor == null ?
Warranty.VOID :
this.sensor.apply(this.extendedWarranty);
  }
  public Article withVisibleDamage() {
    return new Article(Warranty.VOID,
this.expressWarranty,
this.effectiveExpressWarranty,
              this.sensor,
this.extendedWarranty);
  }
  public Article notOperational() {
    return new
Article(this.moneyBackGuarantee,
this.expressWarranty, this.expressWarranty,
              this.sensor,
this.extendedWarranty);
  }
  public Article install(Part sensor,
Warranty extendedWarranty) {   // 1
    return new
Article(this.moneyBackGuarantee,
this.expressWarranty,
this.effectiveExpressWarranty,
          sensor, extendedWarranty);
  }
```

```
    public Article
sensorNotOperational(LocalDate
detectedOn) {  // 2
    return
this.install(this.sensor.defective(detectedOn),
this.extendedWarranty);
    }
}
```

Now back to code Article.java . No matter how nice and simple this code might look, it is the factor. The problem is that the sensor may not be there, which is modeled with a number of reference D referencing the sensor field to mark circuitry defective would result in a now pointer exception. The only situation in which that would be avoided is if install method was invoked first, setting the sensor field to a non null reference. So what do we do to defend from this unfortunate situation?

```
public Article sensorNotOperational(LocalDate detectedOn) {
    return this.sensor == null ? this
        : this.install(this.sensor.defective(detectedOn), this.extendedWarra
}
```

In the best tradition off late 20th century, we would wrap execution into a convenient, if not now instruction. But on the other hand, having to guard against the null in the middle of a class is, to say the least, an embarrassing defeat off. The design can re employ the null object pattern here, like we have done it in the previous module. Well, not really.

Null Object implementation

```
class MissingPart : Part {
    ...
}
```

```
item.install(Part.MISSING, Warranty.VOID);
```

```
public Article install(Part sensor, Warranty extendedWarranty
}

public Article sensorNotOperational(LocalDate detectedOn) {
}
```

✖ Wrong!

```
long sensorsCount = items.stream()
    .map(item -> item.getSensor())
    .filter(sensor -> sensor != null)
    .count()
```

Assume that there exists some now object implementation that can be referenced by this sensor field. What if we wanted to count all sensors installed in the depot? Those now objects would count, too, but they're not really sensors. We don't ask the vendors to transport them to our production plant. That thinking is revealing one interesting fact about substitute objects.

Article.java :

{

Null Object Implementation :

Class MissingPart : Part { .. }

Design which distinguishes substitute objects from the "real" ones is wrong

Design in which objects know there execution context is wrong

```
public Article install(Part sensor, Warranty extendedWarranty) {..}
public Article sensorNotOperational(LocalDate detectedOn) {..}
```

}

If you must know whether an object is real or a dummy, their substitute objects and not the design you're looking for in more technical words, even object must know the context in which it is used. Then now object pattern is not appropriate. Every object must operate correctly in every context in which it is used. Void warranty is an example of an object which can cope with any situation imaginable. Why do I think so? Because it is only exposing behavior. It doesn't make sense to count warranties. Warranties are designed this object into which recall we don't operate on warranty objects, but we delegate calls to them. That is why we don't need to know whether a warrant is genuine or a _____. Sensors are material objects, and we're operating on them. That is the trouble, and sooner or later we will want to know whether we have a sensor or not. This analysis brings us to a conclusion that there is one pro day area in which the design must accept that some objects are playing missing. And that is precisely where many programmers fall back they're using. Now. In this module, I will show you a design which accept this fact. The fact that an object might simply not be there and models it precisely like that. We will introduce optional objects, objects that might be there or might not be there, but they will never be now.

Inventing Optional Objects

```java
public class OptionalsDemo {
    private void display(String value) {
        String printout = value == null ?
"Nothing to show..."
                            : value.toUppercase();
        System.out.println(printout); // print the
string in uppercase
    }
    public void run() {
        this.display(new None());
        this.display(new Some("Something"));
        this.display(new Some("Convert Your
Java Code to Object-oriented"));
    }
}
```

Do you remember the introductory module
when I have mentioned branching around
the Now for the first time? This is that
example and now is the time to make it work
without house The idea Waas to print an
uppercase version off a string.

```java
public class OptionalsDemo {
    private void display(String value) {
        // value string could be missing
(indicated by null)
```

```java
        String printout = value == null
    ?  "Nothing to show..."
                        :
value.toUppercase();
        System.out.println(printout);
    }
    public void run() {
        this.display(new None());
        this.display(new
Some("Something"));
        this.display(new Some("Convert
Your Java Code to Object-oriented"));
    }
}
```

But the problem was that we didn't know if we had the string in the first place. It could be now as well, so the traditional solution would be to branch around the now and choose one print out or the other. It would be dangerous to try to convert the string to upper case before making sure that the references not now. In that introduction, I have already made a point that we could represent this string with an object which suits this uncertainty better. I called that model. I'm maybe string.

```java
public class OptionalsDemo {
```

```java
    private void display(MaybeString
value) {
        MaybeString uppercase =
value.toUpperCase();
        String printout =
uppercase.orElse("Nothing to show...");
    System.out.println(printout);
    }
    public void run() {
    this.display(null);
    this.display(new
Some("Something"));
    this.display(new Some("Convert
Java Code to Object-oriented"));
    }
}
```

Make all calls unconditionally --> Turn
optional calls into calls on optional
objects

This idea is turning the whole situation
upside down because now I am expressing
the thought that there might be a string or
there might be no string at all. Nothing now,
but no string. Can you feel the change when
things are sad that way? Then there is
absolutely no reason to not turn this. Maybe
string into opera case. What would be the

result off this operation. Will it be an uppercase string? Not exactly. The trouble is that we're not certain that we had the string on the input in the first place. On the input, we maybe had a string. So when we turn it to upper case, then we can only maybe have an uppercase string. Do you see that is how optional objects are working. They're optional the way through anyway. We cannot bring to the maybe string. There's no reasonable way to send two cans of something that maybe doesn't exist. We must blood the stream of optional operations with a terminal operation, the one which returns an object which is there for sure. We can do that by supplying a substitute result, but observed, this is the result. It comes at the very end when we need to complete the operation. All objects in the meanwhile, were optional. With this simple idea, we have effectively turned all optional calls into definite book. Unconditional book only made a notional objects. Whether the call will be executed an actual date or not is the question for the ocean object. We don't bother with that. In other words, we have turned optional calls into calls an optional objects.

Before it was my duty to branch and skip the call If it shouldn't be made this time I make calls deterministic lee and optional objects that decides what to do with that. How can we implement this? Maybe string then.

```java
public class OptionalsDemo {
  private static abstract class MaybeString {
    public abstract MaybeString toUpperCase();
    public abstract String orElse(String substitute);
  }
  private static class Some extends MaybeString {
    private String content;
    public Some(String content) {
      this.content = content;
    }
    @Override
    public abstract MaybeString toUpperCase(){
            return new Some(this.content.toUpperCase());
      }
    @Override
```

```java
        public String orElse(String
substitute) {
            return this.content;
        }
    }
    private static class None extends
MaybeString {
        public None() { }
        @Override
        public MaybeString toUpperCase(){
                return this;
        }
        @Override
        public String orElse(String
substitute) {
            return substitute;
        }
    }
    private void display(MaybeString
value) {
            MaybeString uppercase =
value.toUpperCase();
            String printout =
uppercase.orElse("Nothing to show...");
        System.out.println(printout);
    }
    public void run() {
```

```
    this.display(new None());
    this.display(new
Some("Something"));
    this.display(new Some("Convert
Your Java Code to Object-oriented"));
   }
}
```

I will declare a nested class inside this demo
so that you can view all the code in one place
that is not strictly necessary. Dough, maybe a
string is a class is any other. It will expose
the public method to uppercase string, but it
doesn't know how to implement it. Maybe
String doesn't know if there is anything to
turn into. Upper case. I will model that by
turning this glass abstract. The same will be
with thee or else method. This completes the
base class, maybe string. The display
function compiles fine. And now I can start
thinking about concrete implement patients.
Optional objects have two possible
appearances in functional languages. These
air, usually referred to is some and the nun,
some variant will be initialized with content
and none variant will be initialized without
any content. I didn't have to add this
perimeter less constructor I did that to

emphasize the lack of state in the non object. And then comes the implementation. Turning some string Cooper case requires some work. Pick the content, turn it Cooper case, and then wrap that new string into a new some object. Unpacking a some strength to actual string is simple because we already have the string stored inside. The substitute argument is ignored. Implementing the same methods in the non variant will go the other way around. Uppercase. None remains none, but unpacking it plain string means that it has to take the substitute string. None has no string off its own. This completes custom implementation. Often optional string object construction remains missing. I'm not allowed to pass and now reference anymore when there is no strength to display. Then I have to pass a nun. Object ing or regular strings will have to be wrapped into some. It was not the death hard.

```
Main
"C:\Program Files\AdoptOpenJDK\jdk-8.0.202.08\bin\java.exe" ...
Nothing to show...
SOMETHING
MAKING YOUR JAVA CODE MORE OBJECT-ORIENTED

Process finished with exit code 0
```

After all, if I have run this application, you will see that it prints the same content out on the council. But unlike previous design, there's not a single null reference in code, and there is not a single if instruction in code

Advancing from Specific to General Optional Objects

Now that we have seen the working principle, we can try to make this implementation. Maur general. What if we wanted to perform other operations, like turning the string to lower case or a pending to it or calculating a sub string? The list off my wishes is endless.

```
public class OptionalsDemo {
    private static abstract class MaybeString {
            public abstract MaybeString
map(Function<String,String> transform);
        public abstract String orElse(String
substitute);
            public abstract boolean isPresent();
            public abstract String get();
    }
    private static class Some extends
MaybeString {
        private String content;
        public Some(String content) {
```

```java
            this.content = content;
        }
        @Override
        public MaybeString
map(Function<String,String> transform){
            return new
Some(transform.apply(this.content));
        }
        @Override
        public String orElse(String substitute) {
            return this.content;
        }

            public abstract boolean isPresent(){
                return true;
            }
            public abstract String get(){
                return this.content;
            }
        }
    }
    private static class None extends
MaybeString {
        public None() { }
        @Override
        public MaybeString
map(Function<String,String> transform){
            return this;
        }
        @Override
        public String orElse(String substitute) {
            return substitute;
```

```
        }

            public abstract boolean isPresent(){
                return false;
            }
            public abstract String get(){
                throw new
IllegalStateException();
            }
    }
    private void display(MaybeString value) {

System.out.println(value.map(String::toUpp
ercase).orElse("Nothing to show..."));
    }
    public void run() {
        this.display(new None());
        this.display(new Some("Something"));
        this.display(new Some("Convert Your
Java Code to Object-oriented"));
    }
}
```

Why not condense all off them into a single
map method, which receives a
transformation? Concrete implementation in
the some classes? The place where optional
call on the string turns into a call on the
option or string, but none class will skip it
and remain what it is unknown. At the

consuming end, we're witnessing that same conceptual transformation again. The transform method will optionally be invoked on data this is opposed to the ask, then call principal. Optional objects usually allow that start to by offering access to the row content. Some would simply return the content that is easy, but the nun variant will not be able to implement the get the method. There is no way to get the content because there is none. This sub class can only fail. Design based on E's present and get the methods is not consistent in a strongly typed language like Java. Your classes should never allow a call which is bound to fail. This is the ask. Then call principal applied to optional objects and it is no better than branching around now. Don't use this idiom in your code. That is all I have to say about it. This is way better. The code is shorter and it will never cause an exception. This whole effort leads to an ingenious idea. Why maybe string? Why not? Maybe anything

```
import java.util.function.Function;
import java.util.stream.Collectors;
import java.util.stream.IntStream;
public class OptionalsDemo {
    private static abstract class Maybe<T> {
```

```java
    public abstract <TResult>
Maybe<TResult> map(Function<T,
TResult> transform);
    public abstract <TResult>
Maybe<TResult> flatMap(Function<T,
Maybe<TResult>> transform);
    public abstract T orElse(T substitute);
    public abstract boolean isPresent();
    public abstract T get();
}
  private static class Some<T> extends
Maybe<T> {
    private T content;
    public Some(T content) {
      this.content = content;
    }
    @Override
    public <TResult> Maybe<TResult>
map(Function<T, TResult> transform) {
      return new
Some(transform.apply(this.content));
    }
    @Override
    public <TResult> Maybe<TResult>
flatMap(Function<T, Maybe<TResult>>
transform) {
      return transform.apply(this.content);
    }
    @Override
    public T orElse(T substitute) {
      return this.content;
    }
```

```java
    @Override
    public boolean isPresent() { return true;
}

    @Override
    public T get() { return this.content; }
  }
    private static class None<T> extends
Maybe<T> {
    public None() { }
    @Override
    public <TResult> Maybe<TResult>
map(Function<T, TResult> transform) {
        return new None<TResult>();
    }
    @Override
    public <TResult> Maybe<TResult>
flatMap(Function<T, Maybe<TResult>>
transform) {
        return new None<TResult>();
    }
    @Override
    public T orElse(T substitute) {
      return substitute;
    }
    @Override
    public boolean isPresent() { return false;
}
    @Override
    public T get() { throw new
IllegalStateException(); }
  }
```

```java
    private void display(Maybe<String>
value) {

System.out.println(value.map(String::toUpp
erCase).orElse("Nothing to show..."));
    }
    private void
displayAsSquare(Maybe<String> value) {
        System.out.println();
        this.display(this.toSquare(value));
    }
    private Maybe<String>
toSquare(Maybe<String> value) {
        return value.flatMap(this::toSquare);
    }
    private Maybe<String> toSquare(String
value) {
        return this.trySqrt(value.length())
            .map(columns ->
this.toMatrix(value,
(int)Math.ceil(columns)));
    }
    private Maybe<Double> trySqrt(int value)
{
        return value < 0 ? new None<Double>()
            : new
Some(Math.sqrt((double)value));
    }
    private String toMatrix(String value, int
columns) {
        return this.toMatrix(value, columns,
(value.length() + columns - 1) / columns);
```

```java
        }
    private String toMatrix(String value, int
columns, int rows) {
        return IntStream.range(0,
rows).map(row -> row * columns)
            .mapToObj(startIndex ->
value.substring(startIndex,
Math.min(startIndex + columns,
value.length())))

.collect(Collectors.joining(System.lineSepara
tor()));
    }
    public void run() {
        this.display(new None());
        this.display(new Some("Something"));
        this.display(new Some("Making Your
Java Code More Object-oriented"));
        this.displayAsSquare(new None());
        this.displayAsSquare(new
Some("Something"));
        this.displayAsSquare(new
Some("Making Your Java Code More
Object-oriented"));
    }
}
```

we can map and any may be object into
another may be object. Addict speaking off
which we can map to, maybe off any other
type. Ofcourse unpacking the content will
review the object of types of tea. This is the

minimum implementation off a general purpose optional costs. You have similar types in all functional languages. Java has precisely the same class too, and it is called optional. We will come to that in a minute. There is a T least one additional method which is generally useful. That is, when the mapping function returns optional object itself. The map function would return. Maybe maybe the result in this case that is usually not possibly want. And that problem is sold by a more specialized flat map function that get method will also return the Type T code is telling more than words. Let's get to the some implementation. Some becomes some off the its content becomes at the object. Mapping will remain the same Onley expressed in top tea. And here is the flat map. The difference is that flat map doesn't wrap content into a some object flat map can return. A nun that is the novelty and get real also is empty. Non variant will be equally simple. It's map and flat map methods will only return none of the new type. You know, object oriented programming containing complicated concepts almost always ends up wrapping them into a specialized class. So here it is, a specialized class, which models and object which might be missing. The application is still working the same as before. Optional objects are a great idea because they're solving a tough problem in a clean and elegant way. They're also highly compose herbal. You can chain complex transforms in the same way as you would do with streams. Speaking off which optional typing job resembles a stream, an optional object behaves like a stream containing zero or one object before stepping to. More serious examples. I wanted to show you how streams and the options can be mixed together. What if I wanted to print an option of string, inform off a matrix of characters? I can try displaying a proper string. This method is returning another maybe of string. So I helped to use the flat map. This second maybe appears because I have introduced this try square root function. It is sensitive to negative inputs, which produce none off double unknown. A negative input produces a regular square root value. This function returns maybe number of columns in the Matrix. The rest is them straight forward.

These functions are simply turning a string into a major, excusing a stream off sub strings. You can read it in full detail. If you're interested,

```
Main
"C:\Program Files\AdoptOpenJDK\jdk-8.0.202.08\bin\java.exe" ...
Nothing to show...
SOMETHING
MAKING YOUR JAVA CODE MORE OBJECT-ORIENTED

Nothing to show...

SOM
ETH
ING

MAKING
YOUR JA
VA CODE
 MORE O
BJECT-O
RIENTED

Process finished with exit code 0
```

the nun string on Input produces no results. The two rear strings will indeed be formatted into squares and printed out. In this demonstration, you have seen the designing method, which leads to the invention of general purpose Optional objects Lucky for US, job already has this class named optional off the in the next the demo. We will use it to fix deficiencies in the article warranties model

Applying Optional Objects in the Domain Model

```java
import java.time.LocalDate;
import java.util.Optional;
public class Part {
   private LocalDate installmentDate;
   private LocalDate defectDetectedOn;
   public Part(LocalDate
installmentDate) {
      this(installmentDate, null);
   }
   private Part(LocalDate
installmentDate, LocalDate
defectDetectedOn) {
      this.installmentDate =
installmentDate;
      this.defectDetectedOn =
defectDetectedOn;
   }
   public LocalDate
getDefectDetectedOn(){
         return this.defectDetectedOn;
   }
```

```java
    public Part defective(LocalDate
detectedOn) {
        return new
Part(this.installmentDate, detectedOn);
    }
    public Warranty apply(Warranty
partWarranty) {
        return this.defectDetectedOn
== null ? Warranty.VOID
            :
Warranty.lifetime(this.defectDetect
edOn);
    }
}
```

This is the part class again. Some author advised a stick with now inside classes and only to expose no now objects for the public interface. That view might be justified when performers becomes a tough requirement. Otherwise, I insist on proper object modeling code away through.

```java
import java.time.LocalDate;
import java.util.Optional;
public class Part {
    private LocalDate installmentDate;
    private Optional<LocalDate>
defectDetectedOn;
    public Part(LocalDate installmentDate) {
```

```java
        this(installmentDate, Optional.empty());
    }
    private Part(LocalDate installmentDate,
Optional<LocalDate> defectDetectedOn) {
        this.installmentDate = installmentDate;
        this.defectDetectedOn =
defectDetectedOn;
    }
    public Part defective(LocalDate
detectedOn) {
        return new Part(this.installmentDate,
Optional.of(detectedOn));
    }
    public Warranty apply(Warranty
partWarranty) {
        return this.defectDetectedOn
            .flatMap(date ->
partWarranty.filter(date).map(warranty ->
Warranty.lifetime(date)))
            .orElse(Warranty.VOID);
    }
}
```

In that light, the defected attraction date
would be optional. What used to be now in
common references is the cult of static
method empty on optional. What used to be
a plane value is the call to optional off that
was the initialization. And now comes the
prize consuming the optional value This code
reads as follows. Take defected attraction

date, if any, and filter the warranty on that day.

```java
import java.time.LocalDate;
import java.util.Optional;
public interface Warranty {
    Warranty on(LocalDate date);
    Optional<Warranty> filter(LocalDate date);
    default void claim(Runnable action) {
action.run(); }
    Warranty VOID = new VoidWarranty();
    static Warranty lifetime(LocalDate issuedOn) {
        return new
LifetimeWarranty(issuedOn);
    }
}
```

This filter method is new on the warranty interface, and it returns an ocean of warranty. You can look at concrete implementations in warranty classes. They're very simple.

```java
public class Part {
    private LocalDate installmentDate;
    private Optional<LocalDate> defectDetectedOn;
    public Part(LocalDate installmentDate)
{
```

```
    this(installmentDate,
Optional.empty());
  }
  private Part(LocalDate installmentDate,
Optional<LocalDate> defectDetectedOn) {
    this.installmentDate =
installmentDate;
    this.defectDetectedOn =
defectDetectedOn;
  }
  public Part defective(LocalDate
detectedOn) {
    return new Part(this.installmentDate,
Optional.of(detectedOn));
  }
  public Warranty apply(Warranty
partWarranty) {
    return this.defectDetectedOn
      .flatMap(date ->
partWarranty.filter(date).map(warranty -
> Warranty.lifetime(date)))
      .orElse(Warranty.VOID);
  }
}
```

Any warranty valid on the detection date is
converted to a lifetime. Warranty is starting
on the traction day. Otherwise, if there was

no detection date or every extended
warranty has already expired, the overall
result is a void warranty. The part object
will never know whether it is operational or
defective. But the result it produces will
always be correct. No matter what. The
power off optional objects is the same as the
power of streams. Your job is to tell what to
do when there are data and what substitutes
to use when there are no data. And when I
say your job, I mean that your code will not
compile unless you have specified both of the
mapping and the reduction step, compared
this to, if not now called structure, and you
will quickly understand that optional objects
are the safety net.

```java
import java.time.LocalDate;
import java.util.Optional;
public class Article {
    private Warranty moneyBackGuarantee;
    private Warranty expressWarranty;
    private Warranty
effectiveExpressWarranty;
    private Optional<Part> sensor;
    private Warranty extendedWarranty;
    public Article(Warranty
moneyBackGuarantee, Warranty
expressWarranty) {
```

```java
    this(moneyBackGuarantee,
expressWarranty, Warranty.VOID,
Optional.empty(), Warranty.VOID);
  }
  private Article(
    Warranty moneyBackGuarantee,
    Warranty expressWarranty,
    Warranty effectiveExpressWarranty,
    Optional<Part> sensor, Warranty
extendedWarranty) {
    this.moneyBackGuarantee =
moneyBackGuarantee;
    this.expressWarranty =
expressWarranty;
    this.effectiveExpressWarranty =
effectiveExpressWarranty;
    this.sensor = sensor;
    this.extendedWarranty =
extendedWarranty;
  }
  public Warranty
getMoneyBackGuarantee() { return
this.moneyBackGuarantee; }
  public Warranty getExpressWarranty() {
return this.effectiveExpressWarranty; }
  public Warranty getExtendedWarranty()
{
    return this.sensor.map(part ->
part.apply(this.extendedWarranty)).orElse(
Warranty.VOID);
  }
  public Article withVisibleDamage() {
```

```java
        return new Article(Warranty.VOID,
this.expressWarranty,
this.effectiveExpressWarranty,
                this.sensor,
this.extendedWarranty);
    }
    public Article notOperational() {
        return new
Article(this.moneyBackGuarantee,
this.expressWarranty, this.expressWarranty,
                this.sensor,
this.extendedWarranty);
    }
    public Article install(Part sensor,
Warranty extendedWarranty) {
        return new
Article(this.moneyBackGuarantee,
this.expressWarranty,
this.effectiveExpressWarranty,
                Optional.of(sensor),
extendedWarranty);
    }
    public Article
sensorNotOperational(LocalDate
detectedOn) {
        return this.sensor
            .map(part ->
part.defective(detectedOn))
            .map(defective ->
this.install(defective,
this.extendedWarranty))
            .orElse(this);
```

```
        }
}
```

In the article class, The problem was with the sensor field. It was an optional parts, so why not tell it that way in the class text, too? Initially, it will be empty. Not now. Upto, this point of the whole process is the same as in the part class, and public methods will behave similarly. To get the extended warranty we need to apply to a concrete part or else the warranty is considered a void when working with the optional objects. This is the idiom you will repeat every now and then it could get more engaged to dough marking a sensor is defective means the first change, the state of the sensor to defect him and then to install the defective part onto the device. Otherwise, when there is no censor to change in the first place, the whole device remains unchanged. Ofcourse, installing the sensor means the rapidly inside of the optional object. This completes the design, which incorporates optional objects now objects and special case objects.

```
import java.time.Duration;
import java.time.LocalDate;
import java.time.temporal.ChronoUnit;
public class Demo {
```

```java
    private void offerMoneyBack() {
        System.out.println("Offer money
back.");
    }
    private void offerRepair() {
        System.out.println("Offer repair.");
    }
    private void offerSensorRepair() {
System.out.println("Offer sensor
replacement."); }
    private void claimWarranty(Article
article) {
        LocalDate today = LocalDate.now();

article.getMoneyBackGuarantee().on(today).
claim(this::offerMoneyBack);

article.getExpressWarranty().on(today).clai
m(this::offerRepair);

article.getExtendedWarranty().on(today).cla
im(this::offerSensorRepair);
        System.out.println("--------------------");
    }
    public void run() {
        LocalDate sellingDate =
LocalDate.now().minus(40,
ChronoUnit.DAYS);
        Warranty moneyBack = new
TimeLimitedWarranty(sellingDate,
Duration.ofDays(60));
```

```
    Warranty warranty = new
TimeLimitedWarranty(sellingDate,
Duration.ofDays(365));
    Part sensor = new Part(sellingDate);
    Warranty sensorWarranty = new
TimeLimitedWarranty(sellingDate,
Duration.ofDays(90));
    Article item = new Article(moneyBack,
warranty).install(sensor, sensorWarranty);
    this.claimWarranty(item);

this.claimWarranty(item.withVisibleDamage
());

this.claimWarranty(item.notOperational().w
ithVisibleDamage());

this.claimWarranty(item.notOperational());
    LocalDate sensorExamined =
LocalDate.now().minus(2,
ChronoUnit.DAYS);

this.claimWarranty(item.sensorNotOperatio
nal(sensorExamined));

this.claimWarranty(item.notOperational().se
nsorNotOperational(sensorExamined));
    }
}
```

Not a single now, not a single if instruction
No. Four, and while is used anywhere in this
solution, and yet everything is dynamic.

Each of these instructions will follow a different execution path and produce a different outcome.

```
Main
"C:\Program Files\AdoptOpenJDK\jdk-
Offer money back.
------------------------
------------------------
Offer repair.
--------------------
Offer money back.
Offer repair.
--------------------
Offer money back.
Offer sensor replacement.
--------------------
Offer money back.
Offer repair.
Offer sensor replacement.
--------------------

Process finished with exit code 0
```

This was the last demonstration in this book. Let's briefly summarize what we have learned in this module and in the entire book.

Summary

Modeling the missing objects
- Not always possible to use a substitute
- No reason to fall back to using null
- Use optional objects instead
In this module, we have analyzed one very important question. How to model objects

that might be missing. We have seen that it is not always possible nor advisable to devise a substitute objects. We have also seen that there is no reason to fall back to O null references. When an object is missing in this module, we have introduced the optional objects.

Optional object defined
- It is a proper object
- It may contain another object
- Or it may contain nothing
- Forces you to supply both positive and negative scenarios

- All references remain non-null

Optional is a proper object, which either contains another object or contains nothing. It provides a great abstraction, which can be used to implement both positive and the negative scenarios. While working with concrete non null objects all the time
Advanced topics on optional objects
- Optional looks like a stream
- Behaves the same as a stream with zero or one element

- Resulting design is resilient to bugs

In this module, you have learned that usages of functional objects are similar to those of streams. That similarity is intentional as optional can be viewed that the same as a stream of zero or one element. By the end of the module, you have witnessed a re factoring where optional objects were used to produce a design resilience to errors. I hope that this module and the one that preceded have demonstrated that null references are not required in general object oriented programming. This ends this short book .

Avoiding procedural and imperative coding
- Remove branching over Boolean flags
- Use substitutable objects instead
- The runtime type of an object is the live result of a Boolean test
- Branching becomes a call to a virtual method

In this book, we have walked for a set of techniques that can be applied to avoid pitfalls of procedure, imperative coding and rely on objects. Instead, we have seen how branching instructions over boolean conditions can be removed and replaced with substitute hable objects. The runtime type of an object indicates the outcome of a boolean test, and prior branching instruction turns into an unconditional polymorphic called lover trolling method.

Introducing Value Objects
- They are immutable
- They implement value-typed semantic
- Value Objects simplify code

- They help avoid defects

We have been visited. Value objects in

mutability and value that's semantic can be

built into reference types leading to simplify

code and preventing dif checked
Removing null references
- Null Object and Special Case patterns
remove most of the nulls
- Optional<T> type models missing objects
- Introduces a new programming model

In the remaining modules. We have seen how

we can keep away from null references.

Techniques such as now object and special

case objects are helping you eradicate.

Announce almost entirely from custom code

and we're disapprove. Oh, tch falls short. We

have seen how optional type can be used. The

model missing objects. That powerful idea

leads the new programming techniques and

removes the need to Ever use now in your

business related object or in't it code. If these

techniques are new to you, then you can view

This book is the beginning of a search for

better programming practices.

Final Code of Module 3

```java
package com.java;
import
com.codinghelmet.moreoojava.accountstates.
Active;
import java.math.BigDecimal;
public class Account {
    private BigDecimal balance;
    private AccountState state;
    public Account(AccountUnfrozen
onUnfrozen) {
        this.balance = BigDecimal.ZERO;
        this.state = new Active(onUnfrozen);
    }
    public void holderVerified() {
        this.state = this.state.holderVerified();
    }
    public void closeAccount() {
        this.state = this.state.closeAccount();
    }
    public void freezeAccount() {
        this.state = this.state.freezeAccount();
    }
    public void deposit(BigDecimal amount) {
```

```java
    this.state = this.state.deposit(amount,
this::addToBalance);
  }
  private void addToBalance(BigDecimal
amount) {
    this.balance =
this.balance.add(amount);
  }
  public void withdraw(BigDecimal amount)
{
    this.state = this.state.withdraw(
        this.balance, amount,
this::subtractFromBalance);
  }
  private void
subtractFromBalance(BigDecimal amount) {
    this.balance =
this.balance.subtract(amount);
  }
}
package com.java;
import java.math.BigDecimal;
import java.util.function.Consumer;
public interface AccountState {
  AccountState deposit(BigDecimal amount,
Consumer<BigDecimal> addToBalance);
```

```java
    AccountState withdraw(BigDecimal
balance, BigDecimal amount,
                Consumer<BigDecimal>
subtractFromBalance);
    AccountState freezeAccount();
    AccountState holderVerified();
    AccountState closeAccount();
}
package com.java;
public interface AccountUnfrozen {
    void handle();
}
package com.java;
public interface EnsureUnfrozen {
    void execute();
}
package com.java;
public class Main {
    public static void main(String[] args) {
    }
}
package com.java.accountstates;
import
com.codinghelmet.moreoojava.AccountState
;
```

```java
import
com.codinghelmet.moreoojava.AccountUnfr
ozen;
import java.math.BigDecimal;
import java.util.function.Consumer;
public class Active implements AccountState
{
    private AccountUnfrozen onUnfrozen;
    public Active(AccountUnfrozen
onUnfrozen) {
        this.onUnfrozen = onUnfrozen;
    }
    @Override
    public AccountState deposit(BigDecimal
amount, Consumer<BigDecimal>
addToBalance) {
        addToBalance.accept(amount);
        return this;
    }
    @Override
    public AccountState withdraw(BigDecimal
balance, BigDecimal amount,
                    Consumer<BigDecimal>
subtractFromBalance) {
        if (balance.compareTo(amount) >= 0) {

subtractFromBalance.accept(amount);
```

```java
        }
        return this;
    }
    @Override
    public AccountState freezeAccount() {
        return new Frozen(this.onUnfrozen);
    }
    @Override
    public AccountState holderVerified() {
        return this;
    }
    @Override
    public AccountState closeAccount() {
        return new Closed();
    }
}
package com.java.accountstates;
import
com.codinghelmet.moreoojava.AccountState
;
import java.math.BigDecimal;
import java.util.function.Consumer;
public class Closed implements AccountState
{
    @Override
```

```java
    public AccountState deposit(BigDecimal
amount, Consumer<BigDecimal>
addToBalance) {
        return this;
    }
    @Override
    public AccountState withdraw(BigDecimal
balance, BigDecimal amount,
                    Consumer<BigDecimal>
subtractFromBalance) {        return this;
    }
    @Override
    public AccountState freezeAccount() {
        return this;
    }
    @Override
    public AccountState holderVerified() {
        return this;
    }
    @Override
    public AccountState closeAccount() {
        return this;
    }
}
package com.java.accountstates;
```

```java
import
com.codinghelmet.moreoojava.AccountState
;
import
com.codinghelmet.moreoojava.AccountUnfr
ozen;
import java.math.BigDecimal;
import java.util.function.Consumer;
public class Frozen implements
AccountState {
   private AccountUnfrozen onUnfrozen;
   public Frozen(AccountUnfrozen
onUnfrozen) {
      this.onUnfrozen = onUnfrozen;
   }
   @Override
   public AccountState deposit(BigDecimal
amount, Consumer<BigDecimal>
addToBalance) {
      addToBalance.accept(amount);
      return this.unfreeze();
   }
   @Override
   public AccountState withdraw(BigDecimal
balance, BigDecimal amount,
                  Consumer<BigDecimal>
subtractFromBalance) {
```

```java
        if (balance.compareTo(amount) >= 0) {

    subtractFromBalance.accept(amount);
        }
        return this.unfreeze();
    }
    private AccountState unfreeze() {
        this.onUnfrozen.handle();
        return new Active(this.onUnfrozen);
    }
    @Override
    public AccountState freezeAccount() {
        return this;
    }
    @Override
    public AccountState holderVerified() {
        return this;
    }
    @Override
    public AccountState closeAccount() {
        return new Closed();
    }
}
package com.java.accountstates;
import
com.codinghelmet.moreoojava.AccountState
;
```

```java
import
com.codinghelmet.moreoojava.AccountUnfr
ozen;
import java.math.BigDecimal;
import java.util.function.Consumer;
public class NotVerified implements
AccountState {
   private AccountUnfrozen onUnfrozen;
   public NotVerified(AccountUnfrozen
onUnfrozen) {
      this.onUnfrozen = onUnfrozen;
   }
   @Override
   public AccountState deposit(BigDecimal
amount, Consumer<BigDecimal>
addToBalance) {
      addToBalance.accept(amount);
      return this;
   }
   @Override
   public AccountState withdraw(BigDecimal
balance, BigDecimal amount,
                Consumer<BigDecimal>
subtractFromBalance) {
      return this;
   }
   @Override
```

```java
    public AccountState freezeAccount() {
        return this;
    }
    @Override
    public AccountState holderVerified() {
        return new Active(this.onUnfrozen);
    }
    @Override
    public AccountState closeAccount() {
        return new Closed();
    }
}
```

Final Code of Module 4

```java
package com.java;
import java.math.BigDecimal;
public final class Currency implements
Comparable<Currency> {
    private String symbol;
    @Override
    public boolean equals(Object other) {
        return other instanceof Currency &&
this.equals((Currency)other);
    }
```

```java
    private boolean equals(Currency other) {
        return
this.symbol.equals(other.symbol);
    }
    @Override
    public int hashCode() {
        return this.symbol.hashCode();
    }
    public Currency(String symbol) {
        this.symbol = symbol;
    }
    public Money zero() {
        return new Money(BigDecimal.ZERO,
this);
    }
    @Override
    public int compareTo(Currency other) {
        return
this.symbol.compareTo(other.symbol);
    }
    @Override
    public String toString() { return
this.symbol; }
}
package com.java;
import java.math.BigDecimal;
import java.util.HashMap;
```

```java
import java.util.Map;
public class Demo {
    private boolean isHappyHour;
    private Money reserve(Money cost) {
        Money finalCost = this.isHappyHour ?
cost.scale(.5) : cost;
        System.out.println("Reserving an item
costing " + finalCost);
        return finalCost;
    }
    private void buy(Money wallet, Money
cost) {
        boolean enoughMoney =
wallet.compareTo(cost) >= 0;
        Money finalCost = this.reserve(cost);
        boolean finalEnough =
wallet.compareTo(finalCost) >= 0;
        if (finalEnough && !enoughMoney)
            System.out.println("Only this time,
you will pay " + finalCost + " with your " +
wallet);
        else if (finalEnough)
            System.out.println("You will pay " +
finalCost + " with your " + wallet);
        else
            System.out.println("You cannot pay
" + finalCost + " with your " + wallet);
```

```java
    }
    public void run() {
        Currency usd = new Currency("USD");
        Money usd12 = new Money(new
BigDecimal(12), usd);
        Money usd10 = new Money(new
BigDecimal(10), usd);
        Money usd7 = new Money(new
BigDecimal(7), usd);
        this.buy(usd12, usd10);
        System.out.println();
        this.buy(usd7, usd10);
        System.out.println();
        this.isHappyHour = true;
        this.buy(usd7, usd10);
        System.out.println();
        int sum1 = 2 + 3;
        Money usd2 = new Money(new
BigDecimal(2), usd);
        Money usd3 = new Money(new
BigDecimal(3), usd);
        Money sum2 = usd2.add(usd3);
        System.out.println(sum1 + " is " +
(Integer.valueOf(sum1).equals(5) ? "" : "not
") + "equal to " + 5);
        Money usd5 = new Money(new
BigDecimal(5), usd);
```

```java
        System.out.println(sum2 + " is " +
(sum2.equals(usd5) ? "" : "not ") + "equal to
" + usd5);
        Currency eur = new Currency("EUR");
        Money eur2 = new Money(new
BigDecimal(2), eur);
        Euro coin = new Euro(new
BigDecimal(2), eur, "de");
        System.out.println();
        System.out.println(eur2 + " is " +
(eur2.equals(coin) ? "" : "not ") + "equal to
" + coin);
        System.out.println(coin + " is " +
(coin.equals(eur2) ? "" : "not ") + "equal to
" + eur2);
        System.out.println();
        Map<Integer, String> amountToName
= new HashMap<>();
        amountToName.put(42, "Meaning of
life");
        Integer key = 42;
        System.out.println(key + " -> " +
amountToName.getOrDefault(key, "nothing,
really..."));
        Map<Money, String> costToName =
new HashMap<>();
```

```java
        costToName.put(new Money(new
BigDecimal(42), new Currency("USD")),
"Cost of life");
        Money cost = new Money(new
BigDecimal(42), new Currency("USD"));
        System.out.println(cost + " -> " +
costToName.getOrDefault(cost, "nothing,
really..."));
    }
}
package com.java;
import java.math.BigDecimal;
public class Euro extends Money {
    private String iso2Country;
    public Euro(BigDecimal amount,
Currency currency, String iso2Country) {
        super(amount, currency);
        this.iso2Country = iso2Country;
    }
    @Override
    public boolean equals(Object other) {
        return other != null && other.getClass()
== this.getClass() &&
this.equals((Euro)other);
    }
    private boolean equals(Euro other) {
```

```java
    return super.equals(other) &&
this.iso2Country.equals(other.iso2Country);
  }
  @Override
  public int hashCode() {
    return super.hashCode() * 31 +
this.iso2Country.hashCode();
  }
  @Override
  public String toString() {
    return super.toString() + " (" +
this.iso2Country + ")";
  }
}
package com.java;
public class Main {
  public static void main(String[] args) {
    new Demo().run();
  }
}
package com.java;
import java.math.BigDecimal;
import java.math.RoundingMode;
public class Money implements
Comparable<Money> {
  private BigDecimal amount;
  private Currency currency;
```

```java
    public Money(BigDecimal amount,
Currency currency) {
        this.amount = amount.setScale(2,
RoundingMode.HALF_UP);
        this.currency = currency;
    }
    public Money scale(double factor) {
        return new
Money(this.amount.multiply(new
BigDecimal(factor)), this.currency);
    }
    public Money add(Money other) {
        if
(other.currency.compareTo(this.currency) !=
0)
            throw new
IllegalArgumentException();
        return new
Money(this.amount.add(other.amount),
this.currency);
    }
    @Override
    public boolean equals(Object other) {
        return other != null && other.getClass()
== this.getClass() &&
this.equals((Money)other);
    }
```

```java
    private boolean equals(Money other) {
        return
this.amount.equals(other.amount) &&
this.currency.equals(other.currency);
    }
    @Override
    public int hashCode() {
        return this.amount.hashCode() * 17 +
this.currency.hashCode();
    }
    @Override
    public int compareTo(Money other) {
        return
this.compareAmountTo(this.currency.compa
reTo(other.currency), other);
    }
    private int compareAmountTo(int
currencyCompare, Money other) {
        return currencyCompare == 0 ?
this.amount.compareTo(other.amount)
        : currencyCompare;
    }
    @Override
    public String toString() {
        return this.amount + " " +
this.currency;
    }
```

```java
}
package com.java;
import java.time.Duration;
public interface Painter {
    int getId();
    boolean isAvailable();
    Duration estimateTimeToPaint(double
sqMeters);
    Money estimateCompensation(double
sqMeters);
    String getName();
    double estimateSqMeters(Duration time);
}
```

Final Code of Module 5 & 6

```java
package com.java;
import java.time.LocalDate;
import java.util.Optional;
public class Article {
    private Warranty moneyBackGuarantee;
    private Warranty expressWarranty;
    private Warranty
effectiveExpressWarranty;
```

```
    private Optional<Part> sensor;
    private Warranty extendedWarranty;
    public Article(Warranty
moneyBackGuarantee, Warranty
expressWarranty) {
    this(moneyBackGuarantee,
expressWarranty, Warranty.VOID,
Optional.empty(), Warranty.VOID);
    }
    private Article(
        Warranty moneyBackGuarantee,
        Warranty expressWarranty,
        Warranty effectiveExpressWarranty,
        Optional<Part> sensor, Warranty
extendedWarranty) {
        this.moneyBackGuarantee =
moneyBackGuarantee;
        this.expressWarranty =
expressWarranty;
        this.effectiveExpressWarranty =
effectiveExpressWarranty;
        this.sensor = sensor;
        this.extendedWarranty =
extendedWarranty;
    }
    public Warranty
getMoneyBackGuarantee() { return
this.moneyBackGuarantee; }
    public Warranty getExpressWarranty() {
return this.effectiveExpressWarranty; }
```

```java
    public Warranty getExtendedWarranty()
{
    return this.sensor.map(part ->
part.apply(this.extendedWarranty)).orElse(
Warranty.VOID);
    }
    public Article withVisibleDamage() {
    return new Article(Warranty.VOID,
this.expressWarranty,
this.effectiveExpressWarranty,
            this.sensor,
this.extendedWarranty);
    }
    public Article notOperational() {
    return new
Article(this.moneyBackGuarantee,
this.expressWarranty, this.expressWarranty,
            this.sensor,
this.extendedWarranty);
    }
    public Article install(Part sensor,
Warranty extendedWarranty) {
    return new
Article(this.moneyBackGuarantee,
this.expressWarranty,
this.effectiveExpressWarranty,
            Optional.of(sensor),
extendedWarranty);
    }
```

```java
    public Article
sensorNotOperational(LocalDate
detectedOn) {
    return this.sensor
        .map(part ->
part.defective(detectedOn))
        .map(defective ->
this.install(defective,
this.extendedWarranty))
        .orElse(this);
    }
}
package com.java;
import java.time.Duration;
import java.time.LocalDate;
import java.time.temporal.ChronoUnit;
public class Demo {
    private void offerMoneyBack() {
        System.out.println("Offer money
back.");
    }
    private void offerRepair() {
        System.out.println("Offer repair.");
    }
    private void offerSensorRepair() {
System.out.println("Offer sensor
replacement."); }
    private void claimWarranty(Article
article) {
        LocalDate today = LocalDate.now();
```

```java
article.getMoneyBackGuarantee().on(today).
claim(this::offerMoneyBack);

article.getExpressWarranty().on(today).clai
m(this::offerRepair);

article.getExtendedWarranty().on(today).cla
im(this::offerSensorRepair);
    System.out.println("--------------------");
 }
  public void run() {
    LocalDate sellingDate =
LocalDate.now().minus(40,
ChronoUnit.DAYS);
    Warranty moneyBack = new
TimeLimitedWarranty(sellingDate,
Duration.ofDays(60));
    Warranty warranty = new
TimeLimitedWarranty(sellingDate,
Duration.ofDays(365));
    Part sensor = new Part(sellingDate);
    Warranty sensorWarranty = new
TimeLimitedWarranty(sellingDate,
Duration.ofDays(90));
    Article item = new Article(moneyBack,
warranty).install(sensor, sensorWarranty);
    this.claimWarranty(item);

this.claimWarranty(item.withVisibleDamage
());
```

```java
    this.claimWarranty(item.notOperational().w
ithVisibleDamage());

    this.claimWarranty(item.notOperational());
      LocalDate sensorExamined =
LocalDate.now().minus(2,
ChronoUnit.DAYS);

    this.claimWarranty(item.sensorNotOperatio
nal(sensorExamined));

    this.claimWarranty(item.notOperational().se
nsorNotOperational(sensorExamined));
    }
}
package com.java;
import java.time.LocalDate;
import java.util.Optional;
public class LifetimeWarranty implements
Warranty {
    private LocalDate issuedOn;
    public LifetimeWarranty(LocalDate
issuedOn) {
      this.issuedOn = issuedOn;
    }
    @Override
    public Warranty on(LocalDate date) {
      return date.compareTo(this.issuedOn) <
0 ? Warranty.VOID : this;
    }
```

```java
    @Override
    public Optional<Warranty>
filter(LocalDate date) {
        return date.compareTo(this.issuedOn)
>= 0 ? Optional.of(this) : Optional.empty();
    }
}
package com.java;
public class Main {
    public static void main(String[] args) {
        new Demo().run();
    }
}
package com.java;
import java.util.function.Function;
import java.util.stream.Collectors;
import java.util.stream.IntStream;
public class OptionalsDemo {
    private static abstract class Maybe<T> {
        public abstract <TResult>
Maybe<TResult> map(Function<T,
TResult> transform);
        public abstract <TResult>
Maybe<TResult> flatMap(Function<T,
Maybe<TResult>> transform);
        public abstract T orElse(T substitute);
        public abstract boolean isPresent();
        public abstract T get();
    }
    private static class Some<T> extends
Maybe<T> {
```

```java
      private T content;
      public Some(T content) {
        this.content = content;
      }
      @Override
      public <TResult> Maybe<TResult>
map(Function<T, TResult> transform) {
          return new
Some(transform.apply(this.content));
      }
      @Override
      public <TResult> Maybe<TResult>
flatMap(Function<T, Maybe<TResult>>
transform) {
          return transform.apply(this.content);
      }
      @Override
      public T orElse(T substitute) {
        return this.content;
      }
      @Override
      public boolean isPresent() { return true;
}
      @Override
      public T get() { return this.content; }
    }
    private static class None<T> extends
Maybe<T> {
      public None() { }
      @Override
```

```java
    public <TResult> Maybe<TResult>
map(Function<T, TResult> transform) {
        return new None<TResult>();
    }
    @Override
    public <TResult> Maybe<TResult>
flatMap(Function<T, Maybe<TResult>>
transform) {
        return new None<TResult>();
    }
    @Override
    public T orElse(T substitute) {
        return substitute;
    }
    @Override
    public boolean isPresent() { return false;
}

    @Override
    public T get() { throw new
IllegalStateException(); }
    }
    private void display(Maybe<String>
value) {

System.out.println(value.map(String::toUpp
erCase).orElse("Nothing to show..."));
    }
    private void
displayAsSquare(Maybe<String> value) {
        System.out.println();
        this.display(this.toSquare(value));
```

```java
    }
    private Maybe<String>
toSquare(Maybe<String> value) {
        return value.flatMap(this::toSquare);
    }
    private Maybe<String> toSquare(String
value) {
        return this.trySqrt(value.length())
            .map(columns ->
this.toMatrix(value,
(int)Math.ceil(columns)));
    }
    private Maybe<Double> trySqrt(int value)
{
        return value < 0 ? new None<Double>()
            : new
Some(Math.sqrt((double)value));
    }
    private String toMatrix(String value, int
columns) {
        return this.toMatrix(value, columns,
(value.length() + columns - 1) / columns);
    }
    private String toMatrix(String value, int
columns, int rows) {
        return IntStream.range(0,
rows).map(row -> row * columns)
            .mapToObj(startIndex ->
value.substring(startIndex,
Math.min(startIndex + columns,
value.length()))))
```

```java
        .collect(Collectors.joining(System.lineSepara
tor()));
    }
    public void run() {
        this.display(new None());
        this.display(new Some("Something"));
        this.display(new Some("Making Your
Java Code More Object-oriented"));
        this.displayAsSquare(new None());
        this.displayAsSquare(new
Some("Something"));
        this.displayAsSquare(new
Some("Making Your Java Code More
Object-oriented"));
    }
}
package com.java;
import java.time.LocalDate;
import java.util.Optional;
public class Part {
    private LocalDate installmentDate;
    private Optional<LocalDate>
defectDetectedOn;
    public Part(LocalDate installmentDate) {
        this(installmentDate, Optional.empty());
    }
    private Part(LocalDate installmentDate,
Optional<LocalDate> defectDetectedOn) {
        this.installmentDate = installmentDate;
```

```java
        this.defectDetectedOn =
defectDetectedOn;
    }
    public Part defective(LocalDate
detectedOn) {
        return new Part(this.installmentDate,
Optional.of(detectedOn));
    }
    public Warranty apply(Warranty
partWarranty) {
        return this.defectDetectedOn
          .flatMap(date ->
partWarranty.filter(date).map(warranty ->
Warranty.lifetime(date)))
          .orElse(Warranty.VOID);
    }
}
package com.java;
import java.time.Duration;
import java.time.LocalDate;
import java.util.Optional;
public class TimeLimitedWarranty
implements Warranty {
    private LocalDate dateIssued;
    private Duration validFor;
    public TimeLimitedWarranty(LocalDate
dateIssued, Duration validFor) {
        this.dateIssued = dateIssued;
        this.validFor = validFor;
    }
    @Override
```

```java
    public Warranty on(LocalDate date) {
        return date.compareTo(this.dateIssued)
< 0 ? Warranty.VOID
            :
date.compareTo(this.getExpiredDate()) > 0 ?
Warranty.VOID
            : this;
    }
    @Override
    public Optional<Warranty>
filter(LocalDate date) {
        return date.compareTo(this.dateIssued)
>= 0 &&
date.compareTo(this.getExpiredDate()) <= 0
            ? Optional.of(this)
            : Optional.empty();
    }
    private LocalDate getExpiredDate() {
        return
this.dateIssued.plusDays(this.getValidForDa
ys());
    }
    private long getValidForDays() {
        return this.validFor.toDays();
    }
}
package com.java;
import java.time.LocalDate;
import java.util.Optional;
public class VoidWarranty implements
Warranty {
```

```java
    @Override
    public Warranty on(LocalDate date) {
return this; }
    @Override
    public Optional<Warranty>
filter(LocalDate date) { return
Optional.empty(); }
    @Override
    public void claim(Runnable action) { }
}
package com.java;
import java.time.LocalDate;
import java.util.Optional;
public interface Warranty {
    Warranty on(LocalDate date);
    Optional<Warranty> filter(LocalDate
date);
    default void claim(Runnable action) {
action.run(); }
    Warranty VOID = new VoidWarranty();
    static Warranty lifetime(LocalDate
issuedOn) {
        return new
LifetimeWarranty(issuedOn);
    }
}
```

www.ingramcontent.com/pod-product-compliance
Lightning Source LLC
Chambersburg PA
CBHW071110050326
40690CB00008B/1178